Ulsterbus
1967–1988

The Heubeck Years

BUSES IN ULSTER VOLUME 4

Werner Heubeck in characteristic pose in the driving cab
of the first new Leyland Tiger service bus delivered from
Alexander's Mallusk factory in February 1984.
Belfast Telegraph

G Irvine Millar

6 5 4 3 2 1

© G Irvine Millar and Colourpoint Books
Newtownards 2002

Designed by Colourpoint Books,
Newtownards
Printed by W & G Baird Ltd

ISBN 1 898392 81 1

Colourpoint Books are grateful for the generous support of Translink in the production of this book.

Colourpoint Books

Unit D5, Ards Business Centre
Jubilee Road
NEWTOWNARDS
County Down
Northern Ireland
BT23 4YH
Tel: 028 9182 0505
Fax: 028 9182 1900
E-mail: Info@colourpoint.co.uk
Web-site: www.colourpoint.co.uk

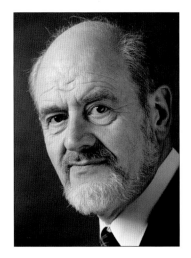

Irvine Millar, a native of Edinburgh, has a wealth of experience in public transport and buses, both from a professional and 'enthusiast' perspective. Moving from London Transport, in 1967 he joined Ulsterbus, with whom he was to be employed until his retirement in 2001, serving successively as PA to the Managing Director, Projects Manager, and Inspector General. Irvine's work, however, has also been his hobby, and to his credit can be listed numerous articles for *Buses Illustrated, Bus & Coach* and *Buses*, as well as the commemorative publication *50 Years of Public Transport*. He is also the owner of a vintage bus, a 1952 Bedford OLAZ. Irvine is married, with two grown-up children, and lives in Belfast.

Front cover: Front cover: 2441 (WOI 2441), one of 600 Bristol RELLs with Alexanders Belfast built body work, which have become characteristic of Ulsterbus and Citybus local bus operations since 1975, at the Wyebridge terminal of service 105 journeys to Lisburn.   *R Bell*

Back cover
Top: 1372 (BOI 1372) prepares to leave Foyle Street, Londonderry for Glasgow on the historic occasion of the launch of the first Cross Channel Express Service to be introduced by the company in June 1970. This new coach was specially equipped with express seating for this purpose.   *Author*

Bottom: 1999 (TOI 1999), a Leyland Leopard with Duple Dominant II luxury coach work pauses at Loch Tummel, Perthshire during an early season management tour in 1979, with Managing Director Werner Heubeck at the wheel.   *Author*

CONTENTS

Foreword

by Werner Heubeck, CBE
Former Managing Director, Ulsterbus Ltd

During the years covered by this book, Ulsterbus operated under difficulties which no public transport undertaking has had to face in Europe, and it is to be hoped that no one will face in the future.

The rundown of the Ulster Transport Authority before its final demise had left it short of capital investment to keep the fleet at a reasonable age, and the shortage of money meant that many of the premises were in a rather unsatisfactory state. Government policy required that Ulsterbus pay its way, and this meant that the money for capital investment had to come from its own resources. This put a very severe restraint on what could be done to provide new buses, and it goes without saying that spending money on premises very much took second place to trying to get as many new buses as the company could finance.

These constraints persisted for many years, but their very severity was a blessing in disguise. It kept the management's feet firmly on the ground and deterred it from the temptation of spending on projects of doubtful economic viability. There is great merit in imposing a very severe constraint on a public utility, and this has been shown to have enabled Ulsterbus to weather quite unbelievable operating difficulties during the years of the Troubles. It is a great pity that the real significance of the example that Ulsterbus had for other undertakings and for the government in London was never appreciated, namely that it is perfectly possible to run a public utility efficiently and above all keep it in that state for many years, not only to the satisfaction of the government but also the travelling public.

Apart from the purchase of 70 Bedford buses in the early days, to do something to provide new buses Ulsterbus standardised on the Leyland 36-foot-long chassis which served the province well. The degree of standardisation was carried to quite extraordinary lengths and very much involved body design as well. Framing sub-components were made identical for different models, and where something could not be fitted in completely, the variation was put into that part of the body which was least likely to be damaged in a traffic accident. Windscreens were deliberately kept split to keep the cost of replacement after accidents or stone throwing to a minimum. Having the bodies built by Alexander at Mallusk was of great mutual benefit and enabled Ulsterbus for many years to put a heavy-duty bus on the road cheaper than anyone else in the United Kingdom managed to do. This policy of standardisation proved its worth when buses were destroyed and helped enormously in maintaining services with a minimum of inconvenience to the travelling public.

The policy did, however, produce a somewhat unglamorous fleet of buses, but that was deemed to be a small price to pay. We had to pay our way, and we did, and our overriding policy was to take our passengers wherever they had to go. We were so busy just coping with our problems that we had no time to participate in the early experiments with minibuses – we were quite content to let others discover how useful they were likely to be. These developments came at the end of the period covered by this book and merit being documented more fully in a later volume.

It gave me a great deal of pleasure that throughout these years we operated the services not only to the satisfaction of the government but, more importantly, to the satisfaction and goodwill of the people who had to use our services.

Werner Heubeck
An Teallach
Longfield
Shetland
January 2002

Preface and acknowledgements

Having been recruited by Werner Heubeck to join the new Ulsterbus management team in January 1967, I have always been conscious of the special privilege of being in at the beginning of a major venture. This added a special quality to the satisfaction I derived from my career in bus operation – so much so that various opportunities offered to me were not sufficiently attractive to persuade me to move away.

I was especially pleased, as I approached retirement, to be asked to compile this fourth volume in the *Buses in Ulster* series, tracing the establishment and development of Ulsterbus operations during Werner Heubeck's directorship. This was also the period of my most active involvement in the company, initially as his 'personal assistant' and then as 'Projects Manager', an unusual job title for a transport concern, which gave me very wide scope, with responsibility for a range of essential functions at head office level, including the fleet, fares policy, publicity and the commercial area. This included all operations extending outside Northern Ireland, such as cross-border and cross-channel scheduled express services and the wide-ranging tours and private hire operations.

I would like to express my sincere thanks to the many individuals who have assisted me with the preparation of material for this book. Werner Heubeck has very kindly contributed a foreword, from his remote retirement in Shetland. Former colleagues such as Sam Thompson and Bobby Campbell have been most willing to stretch their memories to fill gaps in my own, particularly in relation to the changeover from the UTA to Ulsterbus, while Eric Fiddament and Michael McMaster have helped to plug gaps on the engineering side. I have been particularly appreciative of the assistance of John Montgomery, who has been my most able Fleet Control officer for many years, in relation to official fleet records.

Members of the Irish Transport Trust have also been very helpful, especially Howard Cunningham in relation to early Ulsterbus fleet changes, and Will Hughes, who prepared most of the detailed material for the fleet listings.

Thanks to enthusiastic support of the bus photographers within the Irish Transport Trust, who willingly submitted more than 1,000 photographs for consideration, I have had a huge range of views from which to choose. I would particularly mention Raymond Bell, Richard Whitford, Paul Savage, Ian Houston and Howard Cunningham, but all the views selected for inclusion have been individually credited. I also thank the company for allowing the use of old material from the archives, including a number of photographs taken in an official capacity by the late Reg Ludgate, whose personal collection is now held by the Ulster Folk and Transport Museum.

I am happy to acknowledge the generous support which has been given by Ted Hesketh, who succeeded Werner Heubeck as Managing Director of Ulsterbus and who now has the corresponding position within Translink. This has permitted a much greater proportion of the illustrations to be reproduced in full colour than would otherwise have been practicable.

Finally, I would acknowledge the help and forbearance of my wife Irene who, having been married to the bus business for longer than she cares to remember, thought it would all be over when I retired!

G Irvine Millar
Belfast
April 2002

Werner Heubeck
– the man in the driving seat

When the Northern Ireland government at Stormont decided, around 1965, that the Ulster Transport Authority, which had been recording mounting and politically embarrassing losses, should be replaced by a nominal Holding Company with subsidiary companies dedicated to the operation of buses, lorries and railways, they set about a process to recruit managing directors (designate) for each of the companies. It would be the job of the MDs to analyse the existing business and develop plans for the structure and funding of the new undertakings.

The man recruited to take on the bus business was Werner Wolfgang Heubeck, who had no previous association with Northern Ireland and no experience or qualifications specific to the transport industry. How had he convinced the interview panel that he had the character traits and general managerial background and skills to make a success of the task?

Werner Heubeck had been born in 1923 in Nuremberg, the son of an engineer in the city gas works, who progressed to foreman and production manager. Young Werner was fit and healthy, but had achieved no formal qualifications when he was conscripted as a nineteen-year-old in 1942, to serve as a soldier and engineer in the Hermann Goering division within the Luftwaffe. Initially, he served on anti-invasion guard duties in Merignac, in western France, then was moved to Italy, and despatched to join Rommel's North Afrika Korps in the last stages of the campaign in that area. An air attack on the transport

Still youthful! Werner Heubeck as he was photographed at the time of his original appointment as Managing Director (Designate) in 1965. *Ulsterbus*

ships pitched young Werner into the sea, four and a half miles from the African coast, but he not only swam to the coast at Cape Bon, but helped to rescue some of his colleagues – only 60 of the original 550 survived. Captured soon afterwards, he was taken to the USA on one of the last POW convoys, in September 1943, to spend the rest of the war in a work camp in Louisiana. His knowledge of and competence in the English language improved rather rapidly when his compatriots elected him to be the camp interpreter.

A year after the war ended, he was repatriated in 1946, and helped his family to rebuild a bomb-damaged flat in Nuremberg and to provide for a total of nine people, including a homeless elderly couple billeted with his family. He had to source materials for the flat on the black market. Keeping up energy was difficult, as official rations provided less than 1,000 calories per day. After a period working for the US army, organising the transport of armoured vehicles back to the United States, he secured work as a proof reader at the War Crimes Trials, which were being conducted in his home city of Nuremberg. Here he met Monica, from South Wales, who was employed as an interpreter, having studied German and French. In 1949, in spite of major bureaucratic difficulties facing German citizens entering Britain at that time, they came to London to settle and get married. Finding work was not easy, with so many demobbed soldiers, sailors and airmen trying to fit back into civilian life. Having been unsuccessful in London, Werner secured factory work with British Nylon Spinners in Pontypool, South Wales. Starting as a labourer, his determination to work hard sparked opposition from the trades unions, but was noticed by management. Soon he was brought into the technical department where he was asked to write a report on imported material, which attracted favourable attention at a high level. However, further recognition was denied on grounds of his lack of formal qualifications and he was obliged to seek advancement elsewhere. Thus, in 1957, he moved into the paper industry, joining Alex Pirie & Sons at Stoneywood, near Aberdeen, part of the Wiggins Teape group. Here his advancement continued, from Technical Officer through Quality Controller to Technical Manager and finally Mill Manager, as he showed an ability to achieve improved productivity and profit against a background of inadequate investment in a contracting industry.

He recalls that he saw, almost accidentally, the advertisement for Managing Director (Designate) for buses in Ulster, spent a day with the local bus manager in Aberdeen and took a weekend to explore Ulster before the successful interview.

Thus commenced his quite remarkable period of leadership of the bus business in the province, which was to continue until his retirement 23 years later. It could not have been foreseen at that time that his name would gain household recognition throughout the province, nor did he himself expect to remain in the post until his retirement. As the years passed, however, new and challenging responsibilities emerged which maintained his interest. Above all, by responding to the opportunity to be a charismatic leader of the staff through the troubles which beset Northern Ireland through the 1970s and 1980s, he earned the respect of employees as well as passengers, and also those in government and public life with whom he worked to ensure the successful development of the bus operations which had been entrusted to his management. In recognition of his early achievements, Werner Heubeck was awarded the OBE in 1977, to be followed by the award of the CBE for his services to public transport in the Queen's Birthday Honours list in 1988, the year of his retirement.

Aside from work, Werner Heubeck maintained his enthusiasm for physical fitness, with daily calisthenics, jogging runs and leading head office staff on weekly swimming sessions. At one time, he recalls, he was given a very strong reprimand by the police because his jogging route from the Ulsterbus Milewater Road headquarters around the Belfast docks area afforded no security for such a public figure.

He also pursued a wide variety of craft hobbies. At different times he took up copper panel beating, stone carving, knitting Aran patterns (a useful activity to pass the time on the Larne–Stranraer ferry crossings), cabinet making, and wood turning and polishing. It was the latter which was to give him the greatest satisfaction, and for his approaching retirement he built a bungalow and workshop near Glenoe, Co Antrim. His retirement gifts included, rather spectacularly, a huge consignment of well seasoned mahogany. From this workshop, in the ten years following his retirement from Ulsterbus, he turned out hundreds of clocks, table lamps, standard lamps, collection plates and other individually handcrafted wood artefacts and furnishings. He had been commissioned to design and make pieces for numerous churches around Ireland, before he closed up the workshop and moved to Shetland, where one of his three sons works as an

A farewell salute from Werner Heubeck as he steps down from his post as Managing Director of Ulsterbus and Citybus in November 1988, after driving a journey from Dungannon to Belfast on the express service 261.

Belfast Telegraph

ornithologist, monitoring the seabird population around the coasts.

Although often reluctant to speak in public, Werner is a man with very perceptive views on current affairs and management issues, from business through to government and politics, which he enjoys explaining in private conversation.

One feature of Werner Heubeck's character, of which few became aware other than those who directly benefited, was his tremendous depth of human concern. Members of staff who experienced personal problems or family tragedies found his personal counselling and help available far above and beyond the duty of a good employer. In his retirement, this trait was further developed when he found opportunities to provide personal support for a number of elderly and disabled acquaintances, whom he visited regularly and helped to overcome the problems of disability and infirmity.

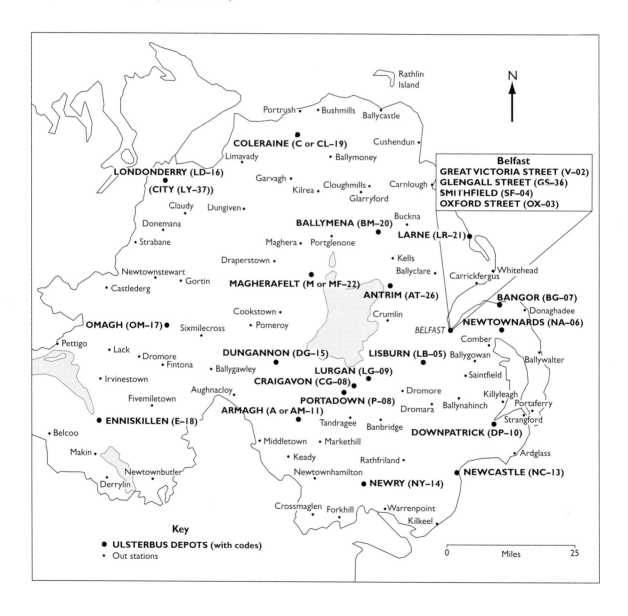

The birth of Ulsterbus

Appointed Managing Director (Designate) in 1965, Werner Heubeck's first task was to investigate the existing business of the road passenger services of the UTA. This study, which included detailed comparisons with operations of the Scottish Bus Group, showed that the UTA bus revenues were comparable to the levels of revenue secured by the Scottish group, even in rural areas, while operating costs in Ulster were significantly higher. It was apparent that the total number of buses operating in Northern Ireland was well below the level which would have been expected for a comparable population, indicating that the development of bus services had been artificially constrained. Fares were generally higher in Northern Ireland, although fares on town bus services were noticeably lower. However, as fares in Northern Ireland had already been frozen for three years, while those in Britain were going up each year in response to inflation, the difference was rapidly disappearing. A very telling comparison related to the utilisation of buses outside peak hours. In Northern Ireland only 20% of buses were used through the working day, compared to 60% in use between the peaks in Scotland. Although partly explained by the number of vehicles used almost exclusively for school transport, this also indicated the paucity of services provided during the day. As the school buses were occupied on average for less than two hours each morning and afternoon, yet were manned by full-time staff earning pay for double that time, there clearly existed opportunities for more economical deployment of staff. This conclusion was confirmed in other comparisons of mileage operated. The study also revealed that a large proportion of the excess costs revealed in the UTA road passenger accounts fell into a heading of 'Other traffic and general charges'. This indicated that the apparent losses of the bus business were largely attributable to allocations of cost from elsewhere in the organisation, a situation which would be avoided in the proposed administration, dedicated solely to bus operation.

Although given the option by the civil servants to 'cherry pick' the most lucrative core business, Werner Heubeck's conclusion, after considering the cost and revenue implications of two alternative levels of cut-off revenue, was that the bus business was inherently viable, and that the best future lay in taking responsibility for the whole business. He succeeded in convincing the designate Board of Directors to support this position.

The designate Board comprised, as Chairman, Sidney Catherwood, who ran successful businesses in the construction industry, and David Wylie, a prominent trades union official. The Board was later strengthened by the addition of Darwin Templeton, a professional accountant, to form a team which remained intact for 18 years, which was quite remarkable for a public-sector business. The Catherwood name was already familiar in the bus industry as his uncle, HMS Catherwood, had been a pioneer busman of the 1920s, developing one of the province's most significant bus undertakings prior to the 1935 nationalisation of the industry,

Werner recalls that the then Minister of Home Affairs, William Craig, "did not believe a word of the final report", but was content to let it proceed "provided they did not have to pour good money after bad". With the Permanent Secretary, Werner secured an undertaking of 'no interference' for two years, in return for a promise that passengers' fares would not be increased. In practice, both undertakings were honoured for much longer. Fares had already been frozen for four years since 1963, under the UTA, due to the impending break-up of that body. The process of franchising some of the 'unremunerative routes' out to other businesses had already commenced, with discussions under way with several prospective parties. These were brought to a stop, except for two groups of routes where negotiations were already past the point of no return, resulting in the formation of the Coastal Bus Service of Portrush, and Sureline Coaches of Lurgan during 1966. Werner said later that had he been appointed six months earlier, he would have prevented even this degree of disruption of the network, not because Ulsterbus was afraid of competition but because he could have maintained continuity of employment and greater security for the staff concerned.

The next major task was to convince the trades unions representing the bus staff, both operating and engineering, that the best future lay in a total commitment to one-man operation and greater efficiency. Werner

Heubeck presented these plans personally to mass meetings of the staff held in the Regal Cinema in Belfast in September 1966. Although major restructuring of companies and even nationalised industries has become commonplace in recent years, this was almost unheard of at that time. Naturally there was great suspicion and even outright hostility to be overcome, but the firmness, with fairness and humanity, with which Werner Heubeck tackled the issues earned him the respect and loyalty of most of the employees, even those whom he addressed as the "cowboys in your midst". It was only after these meetings that the directors of Ulsterbus were able to firm up on the decision to take over the entire undertaking. By December 1966, he issued a notice to all staff describing the steps which had had to be taken, and the progress of work which had been going on behind the scenes since the mass meetings:

I then faced the problem of how quickly could we form Ulsterbus. After some thought we settled on 1st January 1967, as the date. This meant that in four short months work had to be carried out simultaneously and with very few staff along the following lines:

1. Management proposals had to be drafted and submitted to Trade Unions on the conditions of employment that Ulsterbus could offer.
2. Negotiations had to be started with Trade Unions.
3. A Management Structure had to be created which suited Ulsterbus.
4. The posts had to be filled.
5. An accurate estimate of manpower requirements had to be prepared.
6. New schedules had to be cut.
7. The maintenance structure and, in particular, Duncrue Street had to be reorganised.
8. New or even second-hand vehicles had to be bought to the maximum forward commitment that Ulsterbus could possibly stand.
9. The Head Office and central services had to be completely reorganised to ensure that Ulsterbus had regular information on how it was doing.
10. The financial forecast had to be reconfirmed almost continuously to ensure that Ulsterbus would not run into economic difficulties.

The report went on to give comments on progress. Due to a labour dispute with the UTA, the start date had slid back to 1 February 1967. No staff would be asked to work for less than they earned under the UTA, and proposals, still under negotiation, would mean most staff earning more. Financial inducements would apply to staff whose work habits or responsibility changed. Particular difficulties had arisen in placing and recognising the value of clerical staff. Procedures had been agreed with the TSSA. The report continued:

I wish that you who live in the Province could see what is going on at Duncrue Street. Since we separated out bus maintenance there has been a new spirit in the place. This is very encouraging and I hope this will spread to the depots because on this new spirit depends our survival.

I cannot really tell you how much trouble I got into to ensure that we had enough new and even second hand buses in the fleet to take some of the ancient 34-seaters, which cost so much to maintain and look so awful, out of service next year. Since the Directors of Ulsterbus have taken up their posts £550,000 has been committed to the purchase of vehicles and equipment. For an undertaking which has been losing money for five years, this is a pretty good going.

This brings me to a point where I must comment on some of the stories which are going around. I know there are some who say: 'if Mr Heubeck thinks I shall clean a bus for him, he has another think coming to him'. If you are asked, and many of you will be, to clean a bus you will do the best thing you can to make your job secure. If you refuse, many of the services and the jobs that go with them cannot be maintained or taken over. This is inherent in the policy laid down by Government. It has nothing to do with me or my fellow directors. We have found a solution which will make it possible to offer the maximum number of jobs on a full guaranteed week. If this solution is not acceptable we shall form Ulsterbus on a limited scale. The choice is yours, it never has been mine or my fellow directors.

In the last few months the senior staff have not been idle. They have been working hard and for long hours on your behalf. Those of you who pass through Gt. Victoria Street will know that the lights have been burning late at Head Office. So please do not lose patience when we are so near to reaching our goal.

Another aspect of the government plan was that ownership of the bus company, as of the freight company, should be equally shared between the proposed Northern Ireland Transport Holding Company and the existing Transport Holding Company in Great Britain. The Scottish Bus Group had been designated to be the mainland partner for the bus business, on behalf of the THC, but this group pulled out in February 1967, leaving Ulsterbus to remain wholly owned within Northern Ireland.

Against the background history of the UTA, with heavy losses over five consecutive years, the Ulster Bank was persuaded to grant an unsecured overdraft facility of £500,000 at the launch date. Werner recalls that "nobody had faith in public transport", but within eight weeks Ulsterbus had a positive balance.

Originally scheduled for 1 January 1967, the launch date suffered postponement enforced by negotiations with the trades unions, as indicated in the quotation above. Administrative delays, and the need to marshal sufficient buses suitable for one-man operation, necessitated further delays, and Ulsterbus Limited commenced trading on 17 April 1967.

On that day the new duty schedules, with only minor adjustments in frequency and timing, required 1,200 staff, as against the previous 1,600, an improvement in manpower utilisation of 25%, with even greater financial benefits. The basic wage rate for one-man operators went up from £14 3s 3d to £16 0s 0d, and many more of the staff were earning at this rate rather than as basic drivers or conductors. Moreover, the old 34-seaters, described so unflatteringly by Werner Heubeck, had been phased out almost completely. Three months later, the Managing Director issued another information paper addressed to managers:

When we formed Ulsterbus just three months ago we attempted to do overnight something that few undertakings would dream of doing at all. On that day we operated services with about 400 platform staff fewer than we had the day before. This . . . represented an achievement on a scale which, to my knowledge, has never been attempted in Northern Ireland. I think we can all congratulate ourselves on this. However, like so many bold attempts, it left unresolved a large number of problems which are beginning to make themselves increasingly felt now that the first flush is over. As you are the people who, above all others, will have to solve the problems, I am giving you an outline of the situation that is facing us over the next year.

LONG TERM SECURITY OF THE COMPANY

Do not think that Ulsterbus is an efficient operator already. Rather the reverse. There is no doubt that of all the rural operators in Great Britain we are still the least efficient. Over the next 18 months we must increase the surplus we have left at the end of a year by another £300,000 per annum, or nearly by £1,000 a day. If we do not achieve this, the company can only survive on its present scale for a few years at the most. This is a fact of life and we must all face up to it.

A large part of this money will have to come from additional revenue and additional services, or especially, private hire. We are already achieving a good deal of success in introducing new services, but, until we get the fleet into a proper state and more new vehicles, we shall always be somewhat handicapped.

The report went on to detail the problem areas which had been identified in relation to operating costs. These included the rate of accidents and service damage, breakdowns and premature unit-failures influenced by driving practices, problems with heaters, batteries and tyres, poor cleaning standards, excessive overtime and the need for further improvement in manpower utilisation, together with an increasing level of public complaints due to attitudes of a minority of drivers and conductors. The report concluded:

I very much regret that I must address you in this way, when I should by right be congratulating all of you and your staff on your achievements. However, time is not on our side and, for the next eighteen months, we must reach a satisfactory state of affairs.

After that we can all get out of overdrive into top gear. I shall call you together fairly soon so that I can hear how you are doing. I shall also visit all the depots in turn over the next few months so that I can learn at first hand some of your individual problems.

However, despite this stern warning, the basis of a viable commercial operation had been established, and there was a positive balance in the accounts. At the end of the financial year (50 weeks) the Annual Report showed a profit of £278,000, from a turnover of £4,365,000, after provision for depreciation of £334,000. By the following year these figures had improved further, to £400,000, £4,753,000 and £338,000 respectively. The Chairman's Statement in that year made the following comments in relation to corporate targets:

In last year's statement a number of targets were listed and these have either been attained or are still being vigorously pursued. The progress in these directions can be summarised thus:
1. To make the company self sufficient:
This has now been achieved as far as possible and all demands for capital expenditure are being met from our own resources.
 2. To provide good services:
Continued improvement of services has taken place, particularly in the periphery of Belfast. It is our intention to further develop express and other services as suitable vehicles become available.
3. To build up reserves for fleet renewals:
At 30 March 1969, we had cash reserves for fleet and property renewals of some £800,000 after paying for 75 buses delivered during the year at a cost of £480,000.
4. To build a solid company:
The company now gives secure employment to 2600 persons and wages are amongst the highest paid by bus operators in the United Kingdom.
5. To modernise depots:
A contract worth £400,000 has been awarded to McLaughlin & Harvey Ltd. who submitted the lowest tender. The work will commence immediately and should be completed by the spring of 1970.
6. Not to increase fares before 1969:
Our excellent financial results have been achieved without a fares increase. Fares in the province were last increased in 1963 and this, together with the fact that costs have increased annually, reflects very creditably on the company. However, this state cannot continue indefinitely and it is our intention to introduce a fares revision this year. This will cater for the demonetisation of the ½d. and will result in a simpler fares structure, thus easing the burden on the one-man operator. The revision will in some instances mean a slight reduction in fares, and in others an increase. The end result will be approximately £150,000 revenue this year but this will be offset by increased costs.

In the same statement, the Chairman commented and re-emphasised that "if the company is to continue to pay its way it is essential that no sources of revenue available at present will be denied to Ulsterbus". This was no doubt a veiled reference to relations with the Northern Ireland Transport Holding Company to whom no dividend was recommended until the third year of operation.

Business review

Taking a longer-term view of the business, it is by now well known that Ulsterbus was able to maintain a stable and successful out-turn in its financial results throughout the period of Werner Heubeck's leadership. The year end surplus, comprising depreciation charge and net profit, which determined the amount available for reinvestment in new vehicles and improvement of premises, was maintained at around 14% of total turnover, although it fell well below that average during 1973 and 1974, when prices were frozen by government action, and again in 1980.

It was not possible to prevent a progressive decline in overall patronage of bus services. This was a national trend, caused by increasing prosperity and car ownership. Although the Northern Ireland economy may have lagged behind the national trend, the position was aggravated by the worsening civil disorder, which not only discouraged travel, especially for evening social and entertainment journeys, but also physically prevented continued bus operation at such times. Indeed the downturn in revenue during 1971 required the management to undertake substantial economies, with a target reduction of 10% of operations and jobs being set. This was achieved with a reduction of 259 jobs but only 140 redundancies, of which half were short-service employees.

Although there was serious inflation during this period, and fares increases had to be applied in most years, so that revenue would keep pace with the declining value of money, the company was able to show convincingly that these increases had not exceeded inflation, a trend that was noticeable elsewhere, as bus operators tried to offset reduced patronage by raising fares.

The carriage of schoolchildren continued to be a most important component of the business. Indeed the total number of scholars carried on behalf of the education authorities (County Councils until 1973 and Education and Library Boards thereafter) increased every year and, with the decline in other patronage, assumed increasing importance, rising from 17% of all passenger journeys in 1967–8 to 35% in 1987–8.

Ulsterbus business results 1967–1988

Financial year (to March)	Passenger journeys (services)	Total revenue (£)	Net profit (£)	Gross surplus %
1967–68	73.2M	4,365,000	278,000	14.0
1968–69	77.0M	4,753,000	400,000	15.5
1969–70	76.0M	4,891,000	367,000	13.7
1970–71	72.7M	5,411,000	325,000	14.0
1971–72	66.2M	5,966,000	486,000	14.8
1972–73	62.8M	5,873,000	532,000	15.2
1973–74	64.0M	6,074,000	59,000	6.7
1974–75	63.3M	6,439,000	91,000	8.2
1975–76	60.9M	10,407,000	697,000	10.6
1976–77	62.5M	12,498,000	1,982,000	19.3
1977–78	64.5M	13,092,000	793,000	10.6
1978–79	63.4M	15,057,000	1,234,000	13.2
1979–80	62.7M	19,025,000	114,000	5.1
1980–81	60.1M	23,197,000	1,791,000	11.9
1981–82	56.5M	24,514,000	2,176,000	13.1
1982–83	55.7M	26,637,000	2,215,000	12.9
1983–84	56.9M	27,477,000	2,301,000	13.1
1984–85	55.2M	28,230,000	1,181,000	9.5
1985–86	55.4M	30,036,000	2,690,000	14.8
1986–87	50.9M	29,126,000	3,029,000	16.6
1987–88	55.1M	31,845,000	3,865,000	18.9

Development of services

As already indicated, Werner Heubeck's initial investigations into the former UTA bus undertakings were primarily concerned with the underlying economy and efficiency of the operations as they then existed. However, at an early stage he also took on board the potential to develop passenger revenue by improving services. Initially, two types of operation seemed to offer the best prospects. Limited stop or 'express' services across the province had been constrained under UTA management to avoid competition with their railway services; and Belfast peripheral services – between the city centre and the rapidly developing housing estates which were spreading out beyond the historical boundary within which the Belfast Corporation Transport system had retained its legal monopoly.

The way forward for 'express' services had been demonstrated by the encouraging public response to the fast services which had been launched in 1965 under the 'Wolfhound Express' banner to replace the GNR line west of Portadown, to Londonderry via Omagh.

Already a direct express service between Enniskillen and Belfast had grown out of an experimental service operated with a small 20-seat coach connecting with the rail replacement service at Dungannon. It should be remembered that at this time the M1 motorway was still incomplete, with an unfinished section between Lurgan and the Birches (west of Portadown).

Among the first new services to be introduced by the new management team were daily limited stop services between Londonderry and Belfast, one via Limavady and Ballymena, the other via Dungiven and Magherafelt. Again, the M2 motorway was still being built, and very little of the A6 road over Glenshane had been modernised, so these services did well to offer an overall journey time of 2 hrs and 25 or 30 minutes respectively.

Cross-border

Another service which had drawn favourable response from passengers was the long cross-border express service between Londonderry and Dublin, also introduced in 1965, following closure of the GNR railway service via Portadown. This encouraged the new team to explore the possibility of further cross-border cooperation with CIÉ, which resulted in a new limited stop service being introduced by Ulsterbus and CIÉ between Belfast and Galway. The journey time for the 190-mile journey was 5 hrs 45 mins, including a 35-minute break in Cavan, where drivers exchanged vehicles. The service was introduced in June 1967 as a summer seasonal service, but in later years was increased to an all-year operation.

The success of this operation led to further discussions with CIÉ managers, which resulted in new routes and through ticketing being established in 1971 over several corridors. The first new service to result from these talks was 278 Coleraine–Dublin via Mid-Ulster and Armagh, which commenced on 5 April 1971, and extended to Portrush over the summer peak. Through Strabane there was an Aldergrove Airport–Letterkenny service 241, and through ticketing (advertised as service 275) between Belfast and Letterkenny, Ballybofey or Donegal town, through existing services connecting in Strabane. This service was later expanded to include connections through Enniskillen. Another new service was 295 from Dungloe to Omagh, via Donegal town. Service 262 was essentially a through ticketing promotion of existing connections at Enniskillen between the Ulsterbus Belfast–Enniskillen service and the CIÉ Enniskillen–Sligo, Sligo–Ballina and Ballina–Achill Island services.

During this period, Ulsterbus also aspired to operate an express coach service between Belfast and Dublin. Application had been made for the appropriate route licence, not only for the direct route, but also for an alternative scenic route, intended to appeal to the overseas tourists, in the hope that some might be persuaded to come north. These efforts were unsuccessful against the strength of opposition of the railway managements,

A press photographer places Managing Director Werner Heubeck and CIÉ Area Manager (Galway) Ned Fitzgerald at the doorway of the first departure of the Belfast–Galway express coach service on 12 June 1967. The vehicle was Lurgan-based Leyland Leopard/ Potter No 489 (489 TZ), driven by Alan Cunningham.

Ulsterbus

north and south, who feared the introduction of a competitive mode, and who held a dominant position within CIÉ. Twenty years were to pass before these circumstances were to change.

The next significant development of cross-border services followed the establishment by CIÉ in 1978 of the 'Interlink Ireland' network – a range of long and interconnecting services radiating from a central hub at Athlone, in the heart of the 'Midlands' of Ireland. Initially the Belfast–Galway service 270 was used to provide a connection into the Interlink system at Longford. This enabled Ulsterbus to offer connections from Northern Ireland through to Cork, Wexford and Limerick under the heading of service 271. The following year the morning Belfast–Galway service was diverted through Athlone to become part of the Interlink system without a change of vehicle at Longford. Service 270 maintained the afternoon journey from Belfast, balanced by a morning journey from Galway by the more direct route. Initially it was intended that the Ulsterbus vehicle on service 271 would run through to Cork, returning the following day, and balanced by through operation of a CIÉ vehicle from Cork to Belfast. However, this created problems due to incompatibility of vehicles and ticketing systems, and turning of vehicles at Cavan was resumed.

Airlink

Belfast Airport, situated at Aldergrove, about 15 miles north-west of the city, was another potential source of passenger business which the company thought worth cultivating. In the summer of 1969, new express services were introduced linking the airport directly with the north, west and south of the province, rather than expecting travellers to make their way through Belfast. Service 54 (later 239) operated from Rostrevor via Newry, twice daily on weekdays, while service 83 (later 240) from Londonderry via Strabane, Omagh and Dungannon (with connections from Bundoran and Enniskillen) operated twice on Saturdays and once a day Monday to Friday. Service 120A (later 218) between Belfast and Portrush via Antrim and Ballymena had four journeys a day diverted via the airport during the peak summer period. Inevitably the low frequency did not meet all potential passengers' needs, and in the continued absence of significant numbers of incoming tourists, it proved difficult to achieve viability with this operation.

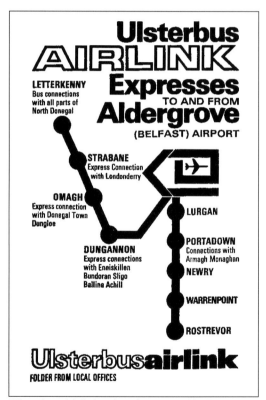

Ulsterbus Airlink advertisement (1971)

Nevertheless, these services continued in varying forms for several years, as managers experimented with routing and timings to reach a wider market.

By 1971 there was a daily service 241 from Aldergrove to Letterkenny, Co Donegal, and return in conjunction with CIÉ. This offered a wide range of connections to the west of Ireland through other new joint services. By 1972–3, direct services to and from Aldergrove were being scaled down and withdrawn in response to the poor returns. However, in 1974 the principal service between the airport and Belfast, which had previously operated 'as required' to connect with specific flights, was relaunched with an advertised timetable offering a regular half-hourly frequency, later trimmed back to hourly during the off-peak period. The last of the direct services was the 239 to and from Newry, withdrawn after the 1976 season.

Cross-channel services

Bord Fáilte, the Irish Tourist Board, also had aspirations to improve facilities for incoming tourists and, conscious that some long-standing steamer services had been withdrawn, initiated a cross-channel coach service between Glasgow and Dublin in 1969. This was operated jointly by Doigs of Glasgow and CIÉ, using the Ardrossan–Belfast ferry. The following year, Ulsterbus and Western Scottish agreed to operate a similar service between Glasgow and Londonderry via the Larne–Stranraer ferry. This was to be the first of a widening range of cross-channel express services introduced by Ulsterbus. Glasgow–Bundoran was introduced in 1971 by the same partners, while in 1974, National Travel was encouraged to turn an existing and long-standing licence for the Stranraer–Middlesbrough route into a jointly operated Belfast–Middlesbrough express service. This licence had originated as the mainland portion of the Northern Ireland Hotel based package tours, for which the UTA and later Ulsterbus had provided coaches.

Early in 1975, the British Rail ferry service between Belfast and Heysham was withdrawn rather unexpectedly. This had been a traditional route for Belfast passengers travelling to Blackpool over the summer months, and Ulsterbus quickly responded with a Belfast–Blackpool express coach service via the Larne–Stranraer ferry. Additional vehicles for the Stranraer–Blackpool operation were hired in from Western Scottish initially, although a variety of other operators were used in subsequent years.

Withdrawal of the Heysham ferry also exposed the weakening of passenger facilities between Belfast and London, and the disparity with major Scottish cities from which London-bound passengers had traditionally had the choice of express coach services as well as day and overnight train services and air services. Accordingly, Ulsterbus, Western Scottish, National Travel and Sealink Scotland agreed a joint operation between Belfast and London, via Birmingham, which commenced as an overnight service in 1976 at a fare of £22 return. In the same year, a joint service was established between Belfast and Glasgow, using the competitive Townsend Thoresen ferry between Larne and Cairnryan.

The following year, 1977, saw the extension of the Glasgow service to Edinburgh, and the introduction of a new joint service between Belfast and Leeds via Manchester, operated with National Travel (East).

Expansion in 1978 included direct connections from Londonderry to Larne Harbour with through bookings to the existing cross-channel services, and a new Belfast–Scarborough/Filey service which was operated throughout by Ulsterbus vehicles provided by the Tours department.

Another very unusual service offered in the summer of 1978 was the 222 between Belfast and Inverness, routed by the new Western Ferries 'Highland Seabird' catamaran service between Portrush and Oban. This was available on Saturdays-only from June to September that year. The following year, Western Ferries diverted their service to Moville instead of Portrush to secure the advantage of being able to offer duty-free sales on board. Ulsterbus offered a Belfast–Moville connection, but the ferry service was badly hit by a postal strike in the Republic which frustrated booking applications, and it was prematurely withdrawn.

Throughout this period, both the Scottish and National bus groups had characteristically guarded their territory and denied Ulsterbus any significant operational responsibilities on mainland Britain. However, the policy of these groups was to change radically following the deregulation of express services in 1980, and the onset of competition over many traditional routes. Ulsterbus pressed home this point very successfully, with the introduction in 1981 of a new Belfast–Bristol express service for which Ulsterbus would be wholly responsible. This operated overnight three times weekly, returning on the following night, and entailed the allocation of a dedicated vehicle to Stranraer depot and the recruitment of locally based drivers. A few years later, when National Express withdrew from the Stranraer–Manchester/Leeds service, Ulsterbus stepped in with a second overnight operation which linked Belfast, via Stranraer, to cities on the east side of the Pennines, including Leeds, Sheffield, Nottingham and terminating in Leicester.

By the end of the period covered by this volume, the total turnover from cross-channel services was nearly £2 million per year, of which more than half was being generated in sales within Northern Ireland. This represented the peak activity achieved, as the business was already beginning to feel the competitive effect of the expansion of domestic air services.

Internal express services

Although much of the express service development has been summarised under the 'Airlink', 'Cross-border' and 'Cross-channel' headings, there were also developments of the internal Northern Ireland network which demonstrated the company's determination to develop new sources of revenue. In 1971, a long-standing summer bus service between Belfast and Portrush, following the picturesque Antrim coast road, was relaunched as express service 252. Reduction in journey time was not a prime objective over this route, although the revised schedule did save 30 minutes out of the almost 4 hr journey, but the changes served to upgrade the image of the service, which I maintain is one of the most attractive scenic journeys in the British Isles.

As mentioned elsewhere, economy measures were sought towards the end of 1971 and these included the

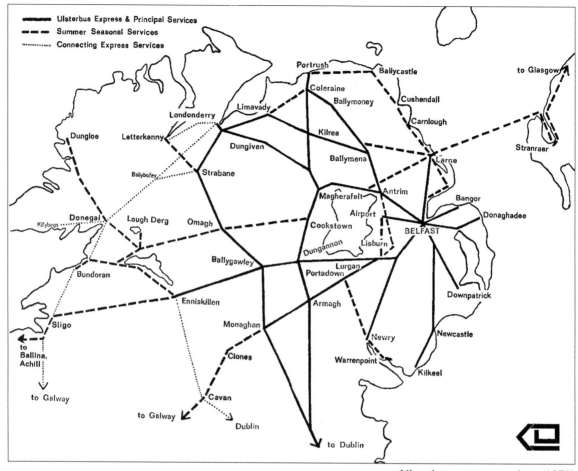

Ulsterbus express services (1971)

reduction of the two direct services between Londonderry and Belfast introduced in 1966, to operate only on Friday and Sunday evenings, for weekend travellers.

In 1976 a new service 221 was introduced between Londonderry and Belfast via Limavady and Coleraine, perhaps encouraged by the closure of Limavady Junction railway station. When Northern Ireland Railways diverted their Derry line trains round by Lisburn into the newly opened Central Station early in 1978, Ulsterbus responded to passenger demands with a new commuter express service between Ballymena and Belfast via Antrim and the M2 motorway, maintaining access to the north side of Belfast and offering a faster journey time.

In 1979 there was another concerted effort to upgrade express services, with services 210/1/5 being diverted on to the M2 motorway and accelerated; substantial frequency increases on 261 (Belfast–Enniskillen) and 273 (Belfast–Londonderry via Dungannon and Omagh); and the introduction of a new service 280 between Cookstown and Belfast via Dungannon and the M1 motorway. Facilities for public transport to and from the cross-channel ferries had also been improved in 1977, with the extension of selected express journeys from the west (Enniskillen and Omagh) to and from Larne Harbour, and in 1979 by the introduction of a service between Coleraine and Larne Harbour. These facilities were additional to the through booked cross-channel services and were designed for casual foot passengers from the ferries who required public transport connections. In general, these improvements were short-lived, there being insufficient tourists around to yield the necessary revenue.

Greater Belfast

As already indicated, Werner Heubeck had identified the Belfast periphery as a potential area for service development. However, the necessary negotiations were to take some time. During the final years of the UTA, Belfast Corporation had negotiated the right to extend their services over several routes in the Glengormley area to the north of Belfast, and to the new Dundonald Hospital in the east of the city. These had been accompanied by the transfer of several routes from the UTA to the municipal operator, which the Authority had assessed as unremunerative. The Corporation Transport system was coming under increasing financial pressure. Having made substantial losses in 1962–4, the profits recorded in 1965 and 1966 may well have been due to the transfer of the Glengormley and Dundonald routes. There was no doubt that the Corporation saw the possibility of extending their operations into more of the peripheral area outside their statutory-defined boundary as potentially highly beneficial to them.

In the new Ulsterbus regime, the validity of the Authority's assessment of route viability as well as the Corporation's enthusiasm for expansion were regarded with suspicion, and there was little inclination to hand over existing Ulsterbus services and revenue. Relationships were not improved when BCT introduced a new service along Kings Road in January 1968, terminating on their boundary on the fringe of the Tullycarnet estate, which was already served by Ulsterbus service 11B. The onset of civil disorder and street violence affected both undertakings, especially in the Belfast area, and it was 1970 before further constructive dialogue took place.

This led to an agreement that Ulsterbus would withdraw its Four Winds service 21, to be covered by an extension of the BCT Ormeau Road service 37, while BCT would withdraw its Tullycarnet service 20 to be replaced by an increased frequency on the Ulsterbus Tullycarnet service, renumbered 21, which would also service BCT bus stops along Kings Road. The situation on the Falls Road was also discussed. Revenue implications for either operator were too great to allow calculated assessment of the revenue and cost effects until experience had been gained of the effect of the more straightforward schemes. The position was further complicated by an ongoing road widening scheme which would require BCT to extend their terminus a significant 400 yards into the Ulsterbus territory. In the event, Ulsterbus was prepared to surrender the relatively new Ladybrook service 186, to be covered by a new BCT service. These changes were implemented on 4 October 1971.

Further changes were implemented on 3 July 1972 when Ulsterbus services 184/5 (Glen Road via Shaws Road and Glen Road via St Teresa's) were withdrawn and replaced by BCT services. This consolidated the control of operations in an area where the political unrest was acute, but the erosion of revenue caused by the 'black taxi' operation was also an important factor in the decision.* Ulsterbus was still heavily involved in the area, having services along Falls Road, and Blacks Road to Suffolk, Twinbrook and Lisburn.

The following year, Belfast Corporation ceased to exist and the Transport undertaking, re-titled Citybus Ltd, was placed under common management with Ulsterbus. However, moves to totally merge the operations were not pursued, and the two legal entities remained. Significant economies of scale were secured rapidly at management level, but staff agreements and management practices were aligned gradually over a longer period.

*The expression 'black taxi' refers to a system of 'paratransit' services which had become established along the Falls Road and Shankill Road arteries in west Belfast during the height of the civil disorder, when operation of the conventional bus services had to be suspended to protect staff and passengers and to try to reduce the destruction of buses. The high-frequency service was run with second-hand London-style taxis, which stopped anywhere to pick up or set down passengers, and was believed to be organised by the paramilitaries. Inevitably, bus patronage and revenues on the routes affected were severely reduced. Belfast Corporation (later Citybus) had been much more seriously affected than Ulsterbus.

Local bus services

Another objective of Werner Heubeck's original report was to seek greater employment of resources during off-peak periods. This was more feasible in urban areas than on rural services. Thus in Londonderry, the frequency of service to the Strathfoyle estate was increased, and new town services introduced in Omagh and Enniskillen in 1968–9. A new town service in Newtownabbey was introduced in September 1969 and shortly after those in Carrickfergus were improved. In Larne, the Antiville town service was revised into a circular to improve efficiency and frequency in November 1970.

In April 1971 there was a comprehensive renumbering of the services, the first major review since the system had been introduced by the NIRTB, around 35 years earlier. As far as possible the traditional numbers were retained for the main services, as were the geographical characteristics of the system. Because of the limitations of the contemporary computer, all services which were distinguished by suffix letters lost these, either being numbered with their 'parent' route or being renumbered. The opportunity was taken to renumber all limited stop and express services in the '200' series.

In September 1971 Londonderry city services were revised, and the traditional cross-town operation was discontinued, due to severe dislocation caused by congestion on the city's only bridge over the River Foyle, as well as the effect of frequent disruption of services due to violence. In the Coleraine area, the two services to Portrush (139 direct and 140 via Portstewart) were combined into a triangular service operated in both directions and fares adjusted so that residents of both Portrush and Portstewart paid the same fare to and from Coleraine either way round. Later that year, new town services were introduced in Antrim, which was being expanded as a 'new town'. A new city service in Londonderry, to the Kilfennan area, started in early 1973.

The escalation of trouble on the streets of Belfast, Derry and other major towns inevitably had a very detrimental effect on passenger travel. This was particularly marked in the evenings, resulting in withdrawal or contraction of late evening journeys on many routes. There were also reductions in frequency on Saturday and Sunday services in most

There had been no tradition of publishing detailed route maps in Northern Ireland under the UTA, so Ulsterbus was breaking new ground when it issued its first Bus Map in 1971. The new map was compiled by local bus enthusiast and journalist Tony Boyce. The cover featured a line drawing of one of the 1968 Bristol LH buses, which was widely used in contemporary publicity.

Bus Map 8p 1971

Ulsterbus

areas due to both the change over from six- to five-day-week working in the early 1970s, and the paucity of passengers at such times.

Operations of Coastal Bus Service of Portrush were taken over in April 1974. This was one of the two independent operators established during the break-up of the UTA. The two main services were renumbered 171 (Coleraine–Ballycastle) and 172 (Portrush–Ballycastle) as the original UTA numbers for these routes had been reallocated in the 1971 renumbering. Later that year, following complaints of inadequate performance, services developed by Sureline Coaches within the Craigavon new town designated area were also taken over by Ulsterbus, although in this case neither vehicles nor the services originally taken over from the UTA were transferred. This allowed Ulsterbus to develop services for the new town on a more comprehensive basis. Revised services and timetables were introduced in the 'new town' area in September 1976, and again with the opening of the new Craigavon depot at Highfield in May 1978.

Further service number changes occurred during 1978, following the introduction of European Drivers' Hours Regulations, due to the need to redefine all local bus services as routes under 50 km (32 miles) in length. Longer-distance express service numbers were not altered at this stage, but required compliance with different rules in relation to drivers' hours.

In the context of rural services, it is worth recording the extension of service 58 (Enniskillen–Aghalane) across the border to Belturbet, in 1968. Destruction of the border bridge left the extension 'temporarily suspended' in the published timetables for almost 30 years, until the bridge was rebuilt! Another border bridge bomb forced the diversion of the 195 service between Pettigo and Belleek to operate over the Boa Island causeway for many years. Another new, albeit very local, cross-border service in the Enniskillen area was service 192, Enniskillen–Swanlinbar, introduced in 1979 following withdrawal of the daily CIÉ service between Cavan and Enniskillen.

Because the rural services operated by Ulsterbus were heavily committed to the carriage of schoolchildren, there was not the widespread withdrawal of rural bus services in Northern Ireland as occurred in England and Wales during the same period. Some withdrawals which did occur were services which had only worked once or twice a week, such as Enniskillen–Florencecourt (Saturdays) and Strabane–Douglas Bridge (Saturdays) which were withdrawn in 1973.

Attention was once again turned to town services in the provincial towns during 1987–8, when the concept of operating new and developed services in this type of urban area with minibuses was explored. This type of operation would allow bus operation to penetrate further into residential areas in an environmentally acceptable form, thus developing attractive town services in areas which had not previously enjoyed this facility, or expanding the scope of such services in towns which had a limited range of services provided by big buses. New services started in Bangor in September 1987. Similar town services in Newtownards followed in February 1988. May saw additional routes in Bangor, a new 'University Link' service between Queens University, in Belfast and Jordanstown, and the introduction of small buses on the Airbus service between Belfast and Belfast International Airport (Aldergrove). In June, a new town service started in Comber, followed in July by a new service between Coleraine and Portstewart, and a seasonal service linking Portrush with its neighbouring caravan sites. Three routes in Derry City started in July, together with a local route based on Dunmurry. Additional town service routes in Newtownards and Coleraine in October concluded the programme for that year, by which time more than 25 small buses were in regular use.

Holiday tours

On its formation, Ulsterbus inherited from the UTA a well-established programme of extended tours covering the length and breadth of Ireland. However, a substantial proportion of the patrons for these tours originated from England or North America, and the UTA had already withdrawn their direct sales effort in these territories as the numbers of bookings did not justify the costs. Ulsterbus realised that the future for this part of the business lay in sales within the domestic market. But to expand patronage from Northern Ireland would require a wider range of tour destinations. Accordingly, plans were laid to introduce a Grand Highland Tour of Scotland in 1968, for which I, with my extensive knowledge of Scotland, was asked to lead the drivers' familiarisation training. Expansion continued with a new tour of Edinburgh, the Scottish Borders and English Lake District commencing in 1970. In that year I assumed responsibility for the entire Tours department, and became personally involved in the ongoing development programme. Planning the annual programmes was always a challenge. New itineraries were needed to maintain the interest of those customers who liked something new or different each year; at the same time the investment in planning and training and the expectation of 'word of mouth recommendation' justified retaining each tour in the brochure for several successive years. Some clients liked to repeat the same holiday and would be disappointed by its replacement by a new destination area. In general, planning for each year's programme started more than a year in advance, while the full commercial assessment of each year's operational results could not be made until about a year later, so that, inevitably, management of the tours programme was a long-term commitment.

A tour of Wales was introduced in 1971, and in 1972 a new Scottish itinerary in the Western Highlands and Oban, together with the first of several 'Scotland's Gardens' special interest tours. Another very popular Scottish itinerary was the Aberdeen and Royal Deeside, introduced in 1974, and destined to have a long run. An ambitious new itinerary for 1975 was Argyll and Skye, which included several of the Scottish internal ferry crossings. An even more ambitious itinerary was the Hebridean Tour, introduced in 1976.

The following year saw a major expansion, with the first foray into continental Europe. This commenced with the early season 'Bulb Time in Holland' tour, which introduced a long association with North Sea Ferries' routes from Hull to Rotterdam and Zeebrugge. There was also a new 'Olde England Tour', which for the first time included London, while the range of tours in England reached the south west, with Devon and Cornwall being offered, initially as an early and late season tour. Scottish tours continued to be refreshed, with Moray Firth and Loch Ness offered in 1978 and the Scottish Borders and Northumbria in 1979.

Following the success of the Bulb Time tour, two main season itineraries in Europe were offered in 1981, covering Holland and Belgium, and the Rhine and Moselle valleys of Germany. After initial problems, the latter became one of the most successful tours operated, remaining in the brochures long after the period covered by this volume. Apart from periodic revision of itineraries within the British Isles, France was the next country to be offered, with a tour of the Loire Valley and Paris starting in 1983. The range of itineraries in Germany extended even further south in 1984, the year of special performances of the Passion Play in Oberammergau, and a new tour featuring the Black Forest. That year also saw the first of a series featuring the Garden Festivals which were being promoted in Britain to revitalise derelict dockland and industrial areas. Continental programmes in 1985 included revised itineraries in Holland and Paris, whilst the 1986 brochure introduced Austria with a 'Lakes and Mountains' tour centred on the famous White Horse Inn on Wolfgangsee. The year 1987 was one of development for the English itineraries, with new tours offered to Isle of Wight, the Cotswolds and East Anglia.

Another feature of the tour brochures during the 1980s was the increasing range of 'short break' itineraries, and early and late season tours, as more and more regular customers showed that they were keen to travel more than once a year with their favourite coach holiday operator!

Brochure illustrations appear on page 146.

THE ULSTERBUS FLEET
The inherited fleet

During the final year of the UTA, when plans were being progressed for the new undertaking, the new management team recognised that the highest priority had to be accorded to expanding the number of vehicles suitable for one-man operation, to replace the large remaining fleet of post-war Leyland Tiger single-deckers, and to commence replacement of Leyland Titan double-deckers.

Although the original planning had envisaged the launch of Ulsterbus on 1 January 1967, for various reasons this date was delayed in stages until the definitive date of 17 April 1967 was settled and achieved. On that date the new company assumed responsibility for all remaining vehicles from the Ulster Transport Authority's fleet. The management structure for the new company was in place by late 1966, and the team appointed were able to ensure an orderly transfer of the fleet. They had identified an official 'operational' fleet of 346 double-deckers and 509 single-deckers from the former UTA, together with 108 single-deckers acquired from other operators during the last few months of the Authority's existence. There was also a large fleet of surplus vehicles for disposal.

All of the double-deckers were post-war Leyland Titans, comprising 46 PD2s with UTA low-bridge bodies, 157 PD2/10Cs with high-bridge bodies built by the UTA on Metcam 'Orion'-style frames (the chassis of these buses had been reconstructed from Leyland PS2 single-decker chassis); and 142 PD3 chassis, also with UTA/Metcam bodywork.

The single-deck fleet also reflected a long-standing adherence to the Leyland marque, although containing batches of vehicles from several other manufacturers. These were supplied in the later years of the Authority's existence and included several demonstrators and prototypes. Of the huge fleet of rear-door Leyland PS1 and PS2 half-cab vehicles which had so characterised the post-war period for both NIRTB and the UTA, only five examples were included in the 'official' fleet, including the two which had been converted to forward door layout. However, 198 other vehicles of this type were taken over, of which 50 were still taxed and may have operated in service during the first few weeks of Ulsterbus operation.

The following is a summary of the official operational fleet acquired:

CHASSIS	QUANTITY	BODYWORK
Leyland Titan PD2	46	UTA Lowbridge
Leyland Titan PD2/10C	158	UTA
Leyland Titan PD3	142	UTA
Leyland Tiger PS1	4	NIRTB
Leyland Tiger PS2	1	UTA
Leyland Royal Tiger	62	UTA 59, Saro 2, B'ham 1
Leyland Tiger Cub	179	Saro 1, UTA 178
Leyland Leopard	6	UTA
Albion Aberdonian	58	Alexander 1, UTA 57
AEC Reliance	76	UTA 70, Plaxton 6
Commer TS3	1	Beadle Integral
Austin J2	1	UTA
Austin T200	3	UTA
Bedford VAS	7	UTA
Bedford SB5	110	UTA 74, Duple 36
Bedford VAL	1	UTA
Leyland Olympic	7	MCW Integral
Leyland Royal Tiger	38	Leyland
Leyland Leopard L1	15	Alexander
Leyland Tiger Cub	48	MCW

It is interesting to note that this list covers almost the entire range of bus chassis suppliers active at that time, with the notable exception of Daimler and Guy (which were standard in the Belfast Corporation Fleet, later to become Citybus under common management), Bristol (which was soon to become a significant supplier) and Dennis (which, having been a major supplier to the former NIRTB, was to reappear in the fleet much later).

Although the Authority had been permitted to purchase very few buses after 1964, the new management team had been allowed to invest in preparation for the change over. The first stage had been to survey the market for suitable second-hand vehicles. A batch of 45 Leyland single-deckers was obtained from Ribble. Of these, 38 were Royal Tigers with Leyland bodywork and seven were the Weymann-built 'Olympic' integral version. All were already 14–15 years of age. These entered service during 1966 but few were repainted in UTA colours, pending decisions over the new livery, the rest operating in the dark red of their previous owner.

Next came a batch of 15 Leyland Leopard L1 coaches with Alexander bodies from Western SMT, which were barely six years old; indeed, one of the batch continued to feature on the front cover of Leyland's sales brochure for the 'Leopard' model for many years. These had been specially equipped for the Glasgow–London overnight express coach service, and with 30 seats and toilets were probably among the most luxurious coaches in the British Isles at the time. These coaches had also entered service in 1966 in their previous owner's black and white livery, quickly earning them the nickname 'Magpies', before they were recalled for repainting and other alterations. Ulsterbus plans were to use these on local services within the province and the superfluous toilets were quickly removed. One of the coaches (No 533) was reseated as a 38-seater with seats recovered from UTA AEC Reliance No 242, which had been wrecked in an accident shortly before the change over. This allowed its seats to be used to bring the remaining coaches up to a 36-seat capacity. Later in life most were reseated again, with bus seats, bringing the capacity up to 41.

The third batch to be sourced also came from Scotland, a fleet of 48 Leyland Tiger Cubs with Weymann bodywork, only seven years old. These had been purchased by Edinburgh Corporation in 1959 as a short-term measure, pending reconstruction of several low bridges on that city's long and intensive No1 circular service. The buses were released for disposal as soon as double-deckers took over the route. With their low gearing, specified for hilly city services, they did not prove to be the most popular vehicles in Ulsterbus, but saw service in many areas. There were all painted into Ulsterbus colours before entering service, and few if any were used in service before 1967.

A limited, although not insignificant, budget was also made available for the purchase of new buses to secure the launch of the new company. Top quality 'heavyweight' models were chosen for long-distance touring programmes and for express services, both activities which were to be extensively promoted and developed. Orders were placed for six 33'/10 m Leyland Leopard coaches with 41-seat Plaxton Panorama bodywork; and seven 36'/11 m Leyland Leopard express coaches with Alexander 'Y' type bodies, built by Potter of Belfast under licence.

For the remainder of the new vehicle order, the priority was to maximise the number of vehicles which could be obtained within the budget available. The choice fell on 70 Bedford VAM 14 chassis with Duple (Northern) 45-seat coachwork. Selection of the Leyland 0400 engine option maintained some connection with the long tradition of standardisation on Leyland products in the inherited fleet. The body style had been developed by Willowbrook, another member of the Duple Group, but with the exception of one pre-production prototype, all of these bodies were assembled at the Duple (Northern) Blackpool factory (formerly Burlinghams), filling a gap in coach orders at the time. One of the reasons for placing the body order with Duple was the promise of delivery in time for the launch of the new company. Indeed delivery dates were critical and the vehicles were pressed into service within days of arrival to ensure that the conversion of duties from crew to one-man operation could be achieved successfully.

As there had been no volume purchases of new vehicles for over three years, these vehicles were very widely used during their first summer season, performing on express services, tours and private hire as well as the basic stage carriage services for which they were primarily intended. After some worrying structural cracks started to appear in the chassis frames, an investigation revealed that in their first six months the entire fleet of Bedfords had achieved twice the average mileage achieved by a fleet of very similar vehicles introduced by Eastern Scottish in the Scottish Borders area at the same time. Happily, the technical problems died away and these vehicles continued to perform a useful function for a full lifespan of 14–15 years.

Fleet renewal

As soon as the trauma of the new company launch was over, work started on a long-term plan for fleet replacement. It was agreed that future vehicle needs would fall into six main categories.

Double decker vehicles would be needed in limited numbers and should be of maximum available capacity, but also designed to be capable of one-man operation. The Leyland Atlantean seemed quite suitable for this application.

A limited number of single-deck buses would be needed for city services, especially in Londonderry. A rear-engined layout was considered ideal as this could offer lower entrance steps and floor levels and would facilitate centre exit doors. Although a variety of rear-engined chassis models had been launched on the market to meet the demand for one-man operation of urban services, it was already apparent that several of these were proving troublesome in operation. The decision was taken to select the Bristol RELL for this application, supported by successful operation of a Bristol demonstrator in Londonderry alongside an AEC Swift. This was a notable decision, since the RELL model had been designed primarily for interurban and rural service operation rather than for city services. But, having been launched in 1962, it had already gained a strong reputation for reliability. Moreover, Bristols had for many years been produced exclusively for companies within the Tilling/NBC group and had only recently become available on the open market, through a marketing and production deal with the Leyland group.

For the more dispersed rural areas it was felt that a lightweight single-decker would be quite adequate. Those available offered the prospect, within 10 m overall length, of 45-seat capacity, generally 10% greater than the oldest single-deckers which they would replace. The added margin of standing capacity under the latest regulations would cater for fluctuation of loadings in peak periods. Apart from the Bedford VAM already purchased, and a Ford equivalent, the Bristol LH model was offered within the Leyland group and could be powered by the 0400 Leyland engine, already well known to the company. The Bristol also offered the underfloor engine position, which gave a quieter ride and a better entrance step layout for one-man operation.

For the bulk of the new single-deck fleet, however, it was recognised that a full size (11 m was the largest vehicle foreseen at that time) heavy-duty chassis would be a wise investment. An underfloor engine would allow for a rear luggage boot, considered essential for the substantial parcels business as well as for passengers' baggage carried on seasonal and longer-distance journeys. That engine position also permitted a good internal layout with all seats facing forward and minimum wheel arch intrusion above the floor, whilst the mechanical specification would allow for up to 24 standing passengers on top of the maximum of 53 seats achievable within the saloon. This type of bus would be able to replace the older double-deckers (59- and 60-seaters) with progressive operational economies, as well as providing additional seats when replacing existing single-deckers on busy trunk routes.

Variations between basic service bus, dual purpose coach and express coach were envisaged simply by varying details of the mechanical and bodywork specification, whilst the same choice of chassis could be completed with a purpose-built luxury coach body for the touring business, thus maximising the standardisation of components within the engineering function. Although other suppliers offered chassis for consideration, the Leyland Leopard was already a very well-established model with a good reputation. This offset the rather limited experience which the UTA had gathered from the small group of Wolfhound coaches which they had purchased in 1965.

When the first batch of Bristol RELLs was purchased for Londonderry city services in 1968, few would have thought that they would be followed by 600 similar vehicles for Ulsterbus and Citybus over the 1975–83 period, many of which are still in service in 2002!   *Ulsterbus*

The plan was to purchase a trial batch of each of these categories of vehicle in the first year, to allow time for service experience and refinement of the specifications, before concentrating on larger volumes in subsequent years of the programme, then conceived as a five year plan. Thus the call issued in 1967 for tenders for 1968 delivery, and the suppliers selected were as follows:

Number and Type	Chassis selected	Other options considered
10 Lightweight dual-purpose coaches	Bristol LH/400 @£2475	AEC Reliance 505 Leyland Tiger Cub
5 Express coaches	Leyland Leopard @£3034	AEC Reliance 691 Bristol RELH680
20 Service buses	Leyland Leopard @£2902	AEC Reliance 691 Bristol RELL600
20 Dual-purpose coaches	Leyland Leopard @£2902	AEC Reliance 691 Bristol RELL680
20 City service buses	Bristol RELL680 @£3275	Leyland Panther AEC Swift 691

Daimler did not submit tenders, although currently offering single-deck versions of their Fleetline chassis, as well as their Roadliner model.

Quotations had also been sought for double-deckers and luxury coaches, mainly to establish the degree of standardisation of mechanical components available from the chassis suppliers, but in these cases no immediate order was intended.

Whilst Ulsterbus had decided very definitely not to continue the tradition of the UTA and its predecessors, of building their own bodywork, it was hoped that that part of the contract at least could be placed within Northern Ireland, to support local industry and employment. This was a policy which the company was to maintain over many years.

On the body side, Potter secured the order by a very narrow margin against Alexander, Duple and Plaxton. It was known that whichever was successful there would be collaboration on design and production capacity between Potter and Alexander. The Potter body for the Ulsterbus contract was a new design specified very closely to Ulsterbus requirements. It was based on the Alexander 'Y'-type cross-section and pillars, although, very significantly, not Alexander's standard 4' or 8' pillar spacing, which produced their characteristic 'short bay' or 'long bay' windows. Potter also produced their own front- and rear-end construction which (unlike Alexander's one-piece fibreglass end panels) was more suited to smaller scale production and Ulsterbus local maintenance needs. Similarly, although windscreen apertures were identical, Alexander only supplied one-piece windscreens, while Potter supplied two-piece split windscreens at Ulsterbus' request. Whilst the Alexander 'Y' type design featured curved glass at the rear, Potter achieved a stylish result with flat glasses, reminiscent of the Duple/Willowbrook design supplied to Ulsterbus in 1967.

These vehicles were ordered in the spring of 1968, for delivery between late 1968 and spring 1969. In fact, at the start of the contract, to meet these demanding delivery schedules, the bodies for the 20 Bristol RELL's were built in Alexander's Falkirk factory broadly to the Potter design, and were designated type 'PU' by that factory.

The ink was hardly dry on these contracts before Ulsterbus, in November 1968, invited tenders for a further batch of ten dual-purpose vehicles, intended primarily to upgrade the Belfast–Airport service. Again Leyland secured the order against competition from AEC with their Reliance 691, whilst on the body side, Potter were again successful against competition from Alexander and Duple. This batch introduced the Leyland O680 engine which was adopted as standard thereafter.

New vehicles under construction: bodywork for new Leyland Leopards under construction in the original Potter factory at Dunmore, Belfast, probably photographed early in 1969.

Ulsterbus archive

Early in 1969 tenders were invited for 76 vehicles comprising the second year of the five-year programme. Whilst these tenders settled that the Leyland Atlantean would be the preferred double-deck chassis against the Daimler Fleetline or the Bristol VR (both VRL and VRT models were on offer at that time), the company's preference for the Leyland Leopard for single-deckers was already firmly established.

Quotations for bodywork had been invited from Alexander of Falkirk, Potter of Belfast, Wright of

Ballymena and Duple of London. Whilst Duple declined to tender for double-deckers, the tender from Wright of Ballymena, which included double-deckers, was remarkable at that time. It was to be some 15 years before Wright would become well established as bus builders nationally, and more than 30 years before they would build their first double-deckers.

Both chassis and body suppliers were aware by now that the company intended these tenders to set a pattern for several years, and prices were based on an expectation of orders for 300–350 vehicles. Knowing of the company's preference for local bodywork sourcing, Alexander of Falkirk strengthened their position by purchasing a controlling interest in the Potter concern, to form Walter Alexander (Belfast) Ltd, and submitting a joint tender.

As indicated, this tendering resulted in a continuous supply situation with 300 Leyland vehicles, including 40 Atlantean double-deckers being delivered from the Alexander (Belfast) factory over the next four years. The single-deckers, all 11 m long, included 20 to 'Express' specification, 140 to the basic 53-seat bus specification and 100 to the more comfortable 49-seat dual-purpose format. These could carry up to 22 standing. In addition to the main contract, six luxury coaches on Leyland Leopard chassis with Plaxton Panorama Elite bodies were purchased in 1971, through the Arlington dealership.

The single-deckers continued the established Potter design and construction, to which Alexander had allocated the type code 'X'. However, the double-deckers were built to a standard Alexander type 'J' design assembled in Belfast from ckd ('completely knocked down') kits manufactured in Falkirk, a process in which Alexander were already experienced for their Hong Kong market.

By 1972, for the next stage of the renewal programme it was time for a major intake of smaller 'rural' buses. Following the lead set by the initial batches purchased in 1968–9, the preferred chassis was the Bristol LH6L and the 10 m Alexander (Belfast) bodies carried 45 seated and up to 22 standing passengers. One hundred of these light and economical vehicles were delivered in 1973/74. A major change in body construction introduced with the Bristol LHs was the replacement of steel by aluminium alloy for the main body frame sections, although this had little effect upon the outward appearance of the finished product. The choice of chassis switched to the Bedford YRQ model for the next 100 lightweight rural buses, delivered in 1974. A batch of 25 of the larger YRT model was also purchased that year, again with the basic bus body specification, seating 53. However, these lightweight vehicles could not be authorised to carry more than eight standing, due to difficulties with the stringent tilt test and no further orders were placed. By the following year Bedford had replaced their YRQ model with the YLQ, with an updated 'blue series' engine, and 50 vehicles of this model were delivered in 1976.

The first two chassis of each of the YRQ and YLQ batches were directed to Duple Coachbuilders to have 41-seat luxury coach bodywork to their 'Dominant' design. One further Bedford YLQ with a Duple Dominant II 45-seat coach body was purchased from dealers' stock in 1978 to replace one of the YRQ Dominants which had been destroyed by fire.

Meanwhile, addition of the former Belfast Corporation bus operations to the responsibilities of the group management (as Citybus Ltd) resulted in a review of the policy in relation to full-size single-deck operations. Although the first order for Citybus was for Leyland Atlantean double-deckers, it was decided that future purchases thereafter would be for standard type single-deckers. The preferred model here would be the Bristol RELL, but now fitted with the Gardner engine, already standard in the Citybus fleet and a firm favourite. It was recognised that this vehicle would also be very suitable for a range of Ulsterbus operations, especially in suburban areas and on routes where luggage capacity was not an issue. This would also give Ulsterbus the benefits of the Gardner engine. As a result of this review, the Bristol RELL took over from the Leyland Leopard as the preferred chassis for the basic bus portion of the fleet renewal programme. However, the Leyland Leopard remained the preferred chassis for dual-purpose, express service and luxury touring coaches. This phase of the renewal programme continued from 1975 until 1982.

During this period a total of 260 Bristol RELL and 337 Leyland Leopards were purchased for the Ulsterbus fleet, together with the 51 Bedford YLQ rural buses already mentioned. Another, more visible, difference in the body specification was adoption of forced air ventilation as a standard feature on all Leyland Leopard and Bristol RELL vehicles from 1975, replacing the sliding window ventilators which had hitherto been fitted on two or three windows on each side of service bus and dual-purpose bodies.

The first batch of 28 Alexander bodies on Bristol RELL chassis for Ulsterbus city services, delivered in 1975, had centre doors, 44 seats and approval for 30 standing, as had the original batch in 1968–9, but the general standard for other Ulsterbus applications was with single door, 52 seats and 24 standing, and 12 of these followed on. Another 15 centre-door vehicles were delivered to Ulsterbus in 1976–7. No further centre-exit vehicles were purchased, as there were by then sufficient to maintain the city services in Londonderry; the use of centre doors in Craigavon and Newtownabbey had proved unsuccessful. Ulsterbus received 115 out of the next order for 150 Bristol RELLs, completed between 1977 and 1979. Another batch of 40 delivered in 1979–80 came from an extension of that contract, covering a further 140 chassis.

Deliveries of Leyland Leopards included 14 with Duple luxury coach bodywork, four with the Dominant I style delivered in 1974–5 and ten with Dominant II style delivered in 1977–9. Ulsterbus also upgraded to the Duple Dominant I body for express service coaches, with four in 1978 and six in 1979. Plaxton were selected by a narrow margin to supply their Supreme luxury coach bodies in 1981, with four express and four touring coaches, of which two were equipped with special features for continental touring, notably a retracting step below the offside door. In 1981 two further chassis, originally earmarked for coach bodies, were made available to Robert Wright and Sons of Ballymena, who, having developed considerable prominence in the market for school and welfare buses, welcomed the opportunity to develop their TT and Royal models for heavyweight chassis to full PSV standards. The first was specified as a 53-seat dual-purpose coach, the second as a 53-seat express service coach.

As already indicated, most of the Leyland Leopards were being specified with the Alexander dual purpose 49-seater body. By 1980, however, the Bristol RELL was becoming difficult to obtain and, with Citybus having been given priority for the available Bristols, Ulsterbus was supplied with a total of 70 53-seat basic service buses on Leyland Leopard chassis, between 1980 and 1982.

Indeed by 1980, Ulsterbus and Citybus were involved in a search for an acceptable substitute for the Bristol RELL chassis, which the Leyland group wished to phase out rather than invest in development necessary to meet stiffer noise and emissions regulations. Ulsterbus had resisted the Leyland National integral vehicle due to loss of the body building contract to the Northern Ireland economy. Leyland therefore offered a chassis version of the National, identified as the B21, which had been intended as an export model. A trial batch of five vehicles was purchased in 1981, with a variety of Leyland and Gardner engines and with Alexander (Belfast) bodies, to which was added a pre-production prototype which had undergone intensive pave testing. All six B21s were subsequently sold on to Ipswich Borough Transport, which had meanwhile acquired the few other vehicles of the B21 type to have been built by Leyland, some of which also had bodywork built by Alexander's Belfast factory.

In the meantime, Leyland had agreed to release a further supply of Bristol RELLs in the form of an extension of 70 chassis to the previous contract, and for their internal reasons reclassified Northern Ireland as an 'export' market. In fact, operators in New Zealand were also demanding continuation of the Bristol RELL model. As the Leyland B21 had not proved sufficiently attractive to secure a bulk order, Leyland conceded a second extension of 70 chassis to Bristol RELL production for 1982. The last 20 of these vehicles were allocated to Ulsterbus and entered service in 1983.

During 1982, Leyland were also poised to launch their new Tiger model to replace the Leopard, especially for the luxury coach market. In order to clear out their chassis stocks for the change over, a batch of 40 Leyland Leopard coach chassis was offered to Ulsterbus at an attractive price and were snapped up as an

This photograph shows the Alexander (Belfast) factory at Mallusk around 1981. In the foreground, a Leyland B21 chassis is being prepared to receive its body underframe. The main production lines include Bristol RELLs, Leyland Leopards, Bedford school buses for the Education Boards and fire tenders for the Northern Ireland Fire Authority. Sam Robinson, Managing Director of the Belfast factory, can be seen in the centre of the picture, discussing production schedules with Jimmy Patterson, Senior Foreman.

Ulsterbus archive

addition to the pre-planned renewal programme. With their power steering and high-performance characteristics, they proved to be the most successful and popular vehicles of their type in the fleet.

Following trials with both Leyland Tiger and Volvo B10M coaches on long journeys from their Scottish base at Stranraer, Ulsterbus decided also to adopt the Tiger for its next batch of luxury touring coaches. The full coach chassis specification was adopted, with 245 bhp engine rating, and the ZF manual gearbox; these were actually the first Leyland Tigers to enter service. In 1983 the company received four 12 m coaches with Duple Caribbean bodywork, featuring major improvements in comfort and facilities for tour passengers, especially for the developing range of continental destinations. There were also two coaches with Duple Dominant IV bodies from dealers' stock, which were purchased primarily for cross-channel express services. These were equipped with Duple reclining coach seats of a design which offered an exceptional level of comfort suited to their prime use on long overnight journeys. Coach purchases in 1984 comprised two further Duple Caribbeans from dealers' stock, four 11 m Duple Laser bodied Tigers and four 12 m Tigers with Wright's Contour bodywork. These marked a major step forward in Wright's production. They had recently entered the luxury coach market with their very striking Contour body on lightweight Bedford chassis and the Ulsterbus order was their first opportunity to build the body on 12 m heavyweight chassis. Two entered service on 12 July that year but the other two, having been delayed at finishing stage, were stored and did not enter service until 1985. These coaches took 57 seated passengers and were intended primarily for local day tours and private hire.

Meanwhile, in February 1984, a unique ceremony was held at the Short Strand Citybus depot, when Alexander formally handed over to Werner Heubeck the last Bristol RELL (of 620), the last Leyland Leopard (of 685), and the first Leyland Tiger for service duty. (The photograph printed on the frontispiece was taken on this occasion.)

As the standard specification of the new Leyland Tiger chassis model was geared to the increasing demands of the luxury coach market in respect of performance, overall weight, speed, and range, Ulsterbus had considered that the standard specification for the Tiger coach chassis was excessive for application to local bus operation. Leyland had responded with a version of the TL11 engine downrated to 170 bhp and driving through the SCG semi-automatic gearbox rather than the ZF manual or Hydracyclic automatic gearbox options offered with the coach chassis. This proved a winning formula, and resulted in Ulsterbus orders over succeeding years accumulating the largest fleet of Leyland Tigers acquired by any operator.

The coachbuilders Alexander (Belfast) had also developed a new body style – the 'N' type – to suit the Tiger chassis. In line with contemporary trends, the shape was more angular and curved windscreens were replaced with flat glasses, angled to avoid internal reflections. This also permitted the adoption of laminated rather than toughened glass. A slight extension in body length permitted the seating capacity to be standardised at 53, whether with dual-purpose or service-bus seat specification. A total of 360 'N' type Tigers were delivered between 1984 and 1988, although production of the same design continued for a further two years after the period covered by this volume. Three batches of ten 'Express' vehicles were purchased, in 1984,1985 and 1988 respectively. These featured revised side-windows at front and rear of the saloon (actually using standard glasses from the body design fitted to Bristol RELLs), which facilitated a distinctive bold-stripe livery. They were also equipped with a much improved design of passenger seating, manufactured by Diplomat specifically for express services.

In 1985, a further two Wright Contour-bodied Leyland Tiger luxury touring coaches were purchased, featuring 49 seats in the shorter 11 m length, intended for the Irish extended tours, together with one 12 m Contour on Tiger chassis, which Wright had built in conjunction with Arlington as a demonstration coach. This retained several features, both mechanical and bodywork, which were not standard to the Ulsterbus specification. These included the fully automatic hydracyclic gearbox (Ulsterbus had opted for the more reliable and economical ZF manual gearbox for its luxury coach Leyland Tigers), together with the livery and 'rainbow stripe' seating fabric. There was also one 12 m coach bodied by Duple with their Laser II design.

In 1986, luxury coach purchases were limited to one 12 m Tiger with Duple 320 body. In 1987 two Leyland Tigers with Duple 340 bodies specially designed for continental operation, and later conversion to higher seating capacity, joined the Tours fleet. There was also one 9 m Volvo B9M with Plaxton Paramount body (the change to Volvo necessitated by the fact that this was the only 'heavy duty' chassis available in 9 m length). This coach was purchased for an Irish Tour operated under contract to NLM, a subsidiary of KLM, the Dutch national airline.

A further attempt by Leyland to sell a rear-engined chassis replacement for the Bristol RELL occurred in 1984–5, when Ulsterbus was persuaded to test a chassis version of the Lynx, which in its complete, integral version had superseded the Leyland National. Alexander (Belfast) built a new body, based on the 'N' type design, and the prototype vehicle entered Ulsterbus service in 1985 after extensive testing. This was followed by a group of six vehicles delivered in 1986 and shared between Ulsterbus and Citybus. Once again, this model did not find favour, and no bulk order was placed. Indeed, like the B21s, these vehicles were also sold off as non-standard vehicles in later years.

This Leyland Titan PD2/10C took the full force of the bomb placed inside Smithfield bus station on 13 April 1972. Needless to say it was not fit to repair and was scrapped along with eight other vehicles which had been parked in the bus station at the time. On this occasion, in the absence of a fire, the bus station was soon put back into use.

Ulsterbus

Second-hand vehicles

With the onset of the 'troubles' in 1968, street rioting, hijacking and burning of vehicles and arson attacks on bus depots became a fact of life for Ulsterbus. 'Withdrawal' of buses ceased to be totally in the company's control and at times, despite the continuous supply contract, the rate of vehicle losses exceeded the rate at which new buses were entering service. It therefore became necessary for the company to look elsewhere for supplies of second-hand buses to top-up the fleet and to maintain a reserve to ensure that it would be able to maintain its full scheduled services after such attacks.

The first major attack on a depot occurred in June 1969 when eight buses were destroyed in Kilkeel. At this time the company examined AEC Reliance buses which were surplus to requirements at Northern General, Gateshead, and similar buses from North Western which were in the hands of a dealer in Salford. After much thought, the view was taken that the purchase of cast-off vehicles could be avoided and the vehicles examined were not purchased.

However, in October 1969, an Alexander-bodied Leyland Tiger Cub coach, NFS No 749, formerly

Edinburgh Corporation Tours coach No 121, which was already in the province for operation for a time with the 6th Ards Scout Troop, was offered to the company and became the first second-hand acquisition. After modification for one-man operation – which included power operation of the entrance door and installation of a destination screen – the vehicle entered service at Magherafelt.

Opportunities were also taken to purchase certain vehicles which had been operated as demonstrators, including one Willowbrook-bodied Ford R192, CNO 797G, in 1971; and one Leyland National, EOI 8060, in 1973.

In 1974, acquisition of the independent operator Coastal Bus Service of Portrush brought in a varied fleet of 18 vehicles. Efforts were made to put these to effective use, although their age and condition meant that only half of the fleet were used in passenger service. Others were useful for spare parts, especially for non-standard types.

Around 1973, reliance upon delivery of new vehicles and extending the life of old vehicles, to replace continuing losses, was eased by a programme of rebuilding the chassis frames of seriously damaged buses, and having new bodies constructed. In total, 29 Leyland Leopards and two Bristol LHs were rebodied between 1973 and 1979, and two Bristol RELLs were similarly treated in 1983. However, refurbishment of chassis had proven to be a very time-consuming job, in an engineering department also under exceptional pressure dealing with vehicles which had suffered repairable damage. When the government 'new bus grants' scheme was found to be payable on new complete vehicles, but not on replacement bodywork, the economic case for rebodying was undermined.

For the most part, therefore, the destruction of vehicles had to be made good by extending the lives of existing buses which would have been due for withdrawal under the continuing renewal programme. Inevitably, this meant that fleet average age was increasing and extra work and costs were incurred in maintaining the older buses to the high standards expected for public service. By 1976 it was realised that this situation was no longer sustainable and that a substantial infusion of second-hand buses would be needed, both to maintain the fleet numbers and to allow the oldest vehicles, which were now problematic to maintain, to be retired.

The first major intake of second-hand buses were nine-year-old AEC Merlins from London Transport. These were intended primarily for the Citybus fleet, but limited numbers were allocated to Ulsterbus depots. Twenty-two of this type entered service between June 1977 and April 1978. Most gave two to three years' service with Ulsterbus and nine survivors were transferred to Citybus in 1980. (There had also been short-term loans between the companies to overcome vehicle shortages after major incidents.) These were followed by a large purchase of AEC Swifts from the same source (the Swift, in London parlance, being the shorter version of the model). Again, only small numbers were allocated to Ulsterbus depots where, due to serious problems with their unreliability, their service was shortlived.

As a result of this experience, Ulsterbus set about sourcing more familiar vehicles, based on the Leyland Leopard chassis. Grey Green of London supplied seven coaches with Plaxton bodywork in 1978; Ribble supplied 12 Marshall-bodied dual-purpose coaches in 1979; and Southdown supplied a total of 32 Leopards with Marshall, Willowbrook and Weymann bodies to what was then known as the BET standard design, also in 1979. A further 12 Marshall-bodied service buses, on the shorter version of the Leopard chassis, followed from Ribble in 1980.

Meanwhile, a group of four MCW-bodied Leyland Atlantean double-deckers, originally with British Overseas Airways Corporation, had been purchased through a Yorkshire dealer. These had 54 coach seats, and a huge luggage locker took up half of the lower deck. However, Ulsterbus workshops soon removed the luggage area and coach seating, and installed standard bus seats for 69 passengers. Single-line destination screens were also fitted. These buses entered service in 1979–80 and continued until 1983. Indeed, two survived as driver training buses for a further four years.

Several years later, having once again a need for double-decker buses, mainly for school transport in rural areas, Ulsterbus turned to Strathclyde PTE to supply Alexander-bodied Leyland Atlanteans. A total of 25 buses of this type were acquired over a three-year period between 1982 and 1984. Lothian Regional Transport was the next source, once again of Alexander-bodied Atlanteans, and again a total of 25 vehicles were purchased at the end of 1985. Although topping up the supply of buses held in reserve, these proved less satisfactory in service, and only half of the quantity were actually used in passenger service over the following three years.

Following the unhappy experience of trying to operate the ex-London AECs, especially the Swifts, Citybus had decided to seek out supplies of second-hand Bristol REs as they were now thoroughly familiar with this model, and early examples with English operators were now reaching the replacement stage. This began a lengthy association with NBC companies, including APT, the group's centralised vehicle disposal unit, which brought nearly 200 ECW-bodied Bristols into Northern Ireland. Once again, only limited numbers of these buses were allocated to Ulsterbus. A total of 21, sourced from West Yorkshire, United, Eastern National and Ribble, were placed in service in Derry between 1983 and 1986.

Ulsterbus also purchased a few specialised coaches for its tours and private hire business from the second-hand market. In 1980, when 12-m-long coaches were still rare, Ulsterbus acquired three Plaxton-bodied Leyland Leopards of this length from Grey Green of London, S&M of Benfleet and Wilkinson of Hebburn. These joined the solitary coach of the same length which had been included in the earlier purchase from Grey Green.

At the small end of the scale, Ulsterbus purchased a Duple-bodied Bedford VAS 29-seater in 1973 from Earnside coaches, through dealers SMT Sales & Service of Glasgow. This followed a trial with a similar vehicle hired from the same dealer. Another Bedford VAS with Duple 'Baby Dominant' 29-seat body was acquired from Weatherdair Ltd of Ballywalter when Ulsterbus took over a staff transport contract in 1978, this replacing the earlier Bedford in the tours fleet.

By 1984, Ulsterbus once again had need of a small 10-m-long coach, preferably on a Leyland Leopard chassis, which by this time was a rare combination. Having located and purchased one from Craiggs of Amble, a second of the same batch was sought out and acquired from Procter of Fenton. Both coaches had Plaxton Supreme bodies which had originally been built with centre doors for the very distinctive fleet of Glenton Tours of London. Although front doors had already been fitted, Ulsterbus gave both vehicles an extensive refurbishment to convert them into 'Executive Club Coaches' with 35 seats and tables, in which role they served for several years. One subsequently reverted to 41-seat layout and worked a local service contract in Scotland, then worked the long Omagh–Longford daily express service, while the other served as a driver training vehicle.

In June 1987, upon the retirement of the proprietor, Joe English, Ulsterbus acquired the business of Sureline Coaches of Lurgan. Sureline had been established during the closing phase of the Ulster Transport Authority, with a group of then 'unremunerative' routes around Lurgan, and had survived successfully for almost 22 years. The final service bus fleet of 21 comprised 13 Leyland Leopards and 8 Bristol LHs, all of which had been purchased from Ulsterbus upon withdrawal. These were rapidly withdrawn again, as soon as sufficient current vehicles could be found to maintain the services. In fact only nine, all Leylands, were kept running at all, and the last were taken off in April of the following year. However, the coach fleet was more varied, including two Bedfords, six Fords and one DAF. Bodywork was equally varied, with four Plaxton, two Duple and two Caetano, together with one most unusual body which had been constructed mainly in the company's own workshops, but finished off by Wright. One new Mercedes/Wright minibus, which had just been delivered and had not been operated, was included in the sale. Most of these coaches remained in use initially, although becoming dispersed across the province. However, the non-standard Ford vehicles did not suit Ulsterbus operating conditions and the last of these was withdrawn by 1990. One Bedford survived longer as a driving school vehicle, whilst the flagship of the Sureline fleet, the DAF MB200/ Plaxton Viewmaster, was to give more than 12 years of service to Ulsterbus in various guises.

The final second-hand purchases relevant to this volume comprised eight Leyland Leopards with Marshall 'BET' style bodywork, from Midland Red South, which were not used in public service. One similar vehicle, though-bodied by Willowbrook, came from Clydeside Scottish (although originally with Paton of Renfrew) in September 1988. It came along with groups of manual gearbox Leyland Leopards, with Alexander 'Y' type bodies, purchased only for driver training from Clydeside and Northern Scottish.

Withdrawal of older vehicles

Having surveyed the input of new and second-hand additions to the fleet, it may be of interest to the reader to survey the programme of phasing out of the older vehicles which evolved.

The policy of progressing conversion of crew operation to one-man operation meant that from the outset the replacement of the 204 rear-entrance double-deckers by high capacity single-deckers would be a top priority. Although virtually all of the UTA's large fleet of rear-entrance single-deckers had already been displaced by the date when Ulsterbus actually commenced trading, there remained a number of non-standard single-deckers, particularly those unsuitable for one-man operation due to lack of power operated doors, which also required priority attention. Thereafter the intention was to update and modernise the operational fleet progressively, in sequence of age, with the objective of achieving a vehicle life range of 14–16 years (that is to say a fleet average age below eight years). Even in 1967, the Leyland Royal Tigers from 1951–2 had already reached that target age, and it was recognised that it would take some years of continuous fleet renewal before these two major priorities could be achieved. And that by an undertaking which had not yet established its commercial capability to generate sufficient funds to support that level of reinvestment!

In the event, the withdrawal of the low-bridge double-deckers was achieved by summer 1969, apart from fleet No 956 which survived for one further year to operate services through a low bridge at Muckamore. Withdrawal of the high-bridge PD2/10Cs progressed steadily from 1969 onwards, until the last day of operation of these half-cab, exposed-radiator, rear-doorway double-deckers was celebrated with special tickets and publicity on 30 December 1972. By this stage, Nos 641, 642, 707 and 727 were the only four buses of the type left. Although dating on paper from 1956–8, these buses had been converted from Leyland PS2 single-deckers delivered in 1948–9.

Among the non-standard single-deckers, the few remaining Leyland PS1s, the Austins, the Commer and the ex-Erne Leyland Royal Tigers without driver-controlled platform doors, were phased out during the first two years of operation. By this time, selective withdrawals of ex-UTA and ex-Ribble Leyland Royal Tigers had also occurred, although some of the ex-UTA type survived until 1972. The last of the ex-Ribble group, No 9008, lasted until February 1974, by then 22 years of age. Many of this type were retained for use as towing vehicles until 1980.

The Bedford SB5/Duple Bella Vega coaches were also unsuitable for service duties, having neither power operated doors nor heaters, although a few had heaters fitted later. The hotel-based tours contracts, for which they had been purchased in 1963, steadily diminished due to the depressive effects of the Troubles on incoming tourism, as well as the rising popularity of package holidays. Ulsterbus tried to find other productive work for the coaches, which at least would release fleet buses for service work, and a number were used on local coaching and contract hire work. In 1973, ten were hired to CIÉ for the summer to help overcome a vehicle shortage, before being sold to an English dealer. Others remained in the fleet until 1975, having been fitted out with salvaged bus seats.

Early in 1972, selective one-man operation of the Leyland PD3 double-deckers had commenced, and this spread steadily over the next four years. In fact the conversion of all duties to one-person operation was completed on 29 November 1976. This had the effect of reducing the pressure for replacement of this type of vehicle. Normal replacement of the type commenced in 1973, but continued throughout the decade, with one vehicle, No 821, surviving until early 1980.

The years from 1973 to 1977 saw withdrawals on a broad front of several former UTA types, including Leyland Tiger Cubs, Albion Aberdonians and Bedford SB5s. In the latter case the unpopularity of their cab and entrance layout and poor performance offset their lower age. Over the next three years, withdrawals of the remaining batches from the ex-UTA fleet continued, so that by the end of the decade the inherited fleet had been largely replaced. The last examples of each of the principal UTA and inherited types to operate in normal service were:

Bus	Number/Dates
Albion Aberdonian:	113, April 1976
Bedford SB5 school buses:	126, June 1975
Bedford SB5/ Duple coaches;	167, August 1975
Leyland Tiger Cub PSUC1/5T:	406, December 1978
Leyland Tiger Cub PSUC1/12:	439, 458, 474, 480, June 1980
Leyland Tiger Cub PSUC1/3 (ex-Edinburgh):	1006, March 1976. (1039, September 1977, after transfer to Citybus)
AEC Reliance:	234, 235, 236, 251, June 1980.
Leyland Leopard L1 (ex- Western SMT):	540, February 1981

Appropriately, the last vehicle to be built by the UTA was also to be the last of such vehicles to operate in Ulsterbus service. Leyland Leopard (Wolfhound express coach) No 486 of 1966 was withdrawn from passenger service late in 1980 for conversion for towing duties, in which capacity it survived until 1982 when it was destroyed in an attack on Armagh depot. Several of each batch of Leyland Tiger Cubs were sold on to the Lough Swilly fleet for further use, while a number of Tiger Cubs and many of the 'Western' Leopards replaced the ex-Ribble Royal Tigers as towing vehicles to give many more years' useful work.

Although many had been destroyed already, 'normal' withdrawal of the Bedford VAM/Duple buses, bought to launch the new company, had begun by 1978 and continued over the next three years, the last vehicle being No 1203, withdrawn in February 1981. Nine of these were sold to Lough Swilly for further use. The attrition rate among the 1967 Leyland Leopards had been high, but the survivors, by then regarded as 'non-standard', were phased out in 1980, when three with Potter bodies and two with Plaxton bodies passed to Lough Swilly, leaving one Plaxton-bodied example to function as a towing vehicle.

By this time, it can be seen that the vehicle age target was being achieved – the loss of many younger vehicles by malicious action was partly offset by the second-hand acquisitions.

This progress was maintained throughout the 1980s, with vehicles purchased by the company between 1968 and 1972 being withdrawn generally within 14–16 years. The Bristol LH6Ls of 1968 were withdrawn in 1980, and the sole survivor of the 1969 Bristol RELL6Ls (No 1058) was withdrawn in 1985 and sold for preservation. Among the early Leyland Leopards, likewise, most of the survivors were withdrawn in 1985, including No 1337 which was sold for preservation, but sadly perished in a depot arson attack later. However, a few, remarkably, worked on until 1988, including Nos 1303, 1313 and 1317. The company retained No 1301 for preservation, but the project had to be abandoned later due to advanced corrosion.

Most of the Leyland Leopards purchased between 1970 and 1972 were withdrawn between 1985 and 1988. The longest survivors were Nos 1559, 1573 and 1578 which worked on into 1989, the last mentioned being withdrawn in August of that year. One of the type (No 1512) survived much longer as a depot towcar.

Bristol LH6Ls of 1973 delivery were being phased out between 1984 and 1988. One of the last was No 1629 (November 1988) which has been preserved.

The Bedford YRTs of 1974, having proved less satisfactory in service than the shorter YRQs, were withdrawn between 1980 and 1983, while the YRQs worked on until 1986–9. The last of these was No 1749, in August 1989. Many of these also became towing vehicles.

With reversion to purchase of 'heavyweight' Leyland and Bristol RELL models from 1975 onwards, the target life of these buses extended beyond the era covered by this volume, and most were still working beyond 1988.

The inherited fleet

Leyland Tiger PS2 No 8858 (MZ 1929), which had been extended and equipped with a forward entrance door and extra seats by the UTA, was the only half-cab single-decker repainted by Ulsterbus for service operation. This was for Londonderry city services, which remained crew operated at the time. It is seen here on a warm day in August 1967 during layover at the Lone Moor terminus. *H Cunningham*

Of the two Royal Tigers which had been former UTA luxury coaches, No 8930 did not survive long enough to be repainted, but No 8931 (MZ 7966) lasted four years in Ulsterbus livery. *H Cunningham*

Ulsterbus inherited 59 of these robust, if heavyweight, Leyland Royal Tigers from the UTA. This vehicle, No 8987 (OZ 860), remarkably had survived for more than four years in UTA colours when it was photographed in Portrush bus station in June 1971.

H Cunningham

Most of the ex-UTA Royal Tigers had their timber roof-racks and their rear ladders removed as a weight-saving measure when being repainted into Ulsterbus livery. Number 8938 (MZ 7973) is seen at Downpatrick late in 1971.

Author

This Leyland Royal Tiger with classic Burlingham Seagull body had become UTA No 205 (IL 7077) when acquired from Erne Bus Service in 1958, and was unique among the Erne Bus fleet in having been painted in UTA livery. It was photographed in North Street bus yard while en route to Duncrue Street workshops for repainting. *Author*

Although its centre door made it quite unsuitable for one-man operation, Ulsterbus considered it suitable for refurbishment as a luxury coach, and it was an early recipient of the new colours when photographed in Glengall Street in May 1967 as No 598 (IL 7077). *H Cunningham*

The Saro-bodied Leyland Royal Tigers, also ex-Erne Bus Service, were also early recipients of Ulsterbus livery, although restricted to contract service due to the lack of power operation of their entrance doors. 8995/6, formerly 203/4, IL 5605/98 are both included in this photograph of contract buses at Narrow Gauge Road, Larne in July 1967. Also visible is the sole Leyland Tiger PS1 which was equipped with a forward entrance, 7845 (GZ 6073) and one of the three Austin T200 20-seaters, 3 (8815 AZ).   *R Whitford*

Although many of the ex-Ribble Royal Tigers acquired in the final year of UTA operation had entered service in Ribble red, this line-up of ex-Ribble vehicles are in full Ulsterbus livery at Newcastle depot in August 1972. The vehicles are from left 9013, 9008, 9026, 9027, and 9025 (respectively ERN 684, ECK 595, ERN 706, 708 and 705).   *H Cunningham*

One of seven ex-Ribble Leyland Olympic HR40s, No 9102 (DRN 116), all of which were allocated to Omagh depot, is seen here on service 92, passing through Gortin Glen, County Tyrone, in August 1970.

H Cunningham

Ulsterbus did not intend to repaint any of the 'low-bridge' Leyland Titan PD2s, as it was expected they would be quickly replaced. However, No 944 (OZ 2131), seen in Coleraine depot in August 1967, was repainted on the insistence of a local PSV inspector.

R Whitford

Most of the 158 Leyland Titan PD2/10C double-deckers were repainted into Ulsterbus colours. A very early repaint was No 716 (UZ 716), showing the large fleet-name and contrasting with No 715 (UZ 715) in UTA dark green, behind. These were photographed in May 1967 in Larne depot.   *R Whitford*

More typical of later repaints is No 617 (WZ 617), photographed on the Bangor to Belfast route in May 1970. Traffic conditions (two 'Minis') make a sharp comparison with conditions today.   *R Whitford*

The official last day of operation of the half-cab double-deckers was marked with special souvenir tickets (reproduced below) and photo opportunities. Number 727 (UZ 7727) was one of the vehicles performing that day (Saturday, 30 December 1972) at Newtownards bus station, under the watchful eye of Inspector Pat Gilmore.

H Cunningham

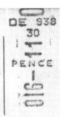

THE END OF AN ERA
Issued to commemorate the last scheduled day of operation of Leyland P.D.2 double deck vehicles with 'half cabs' and rear platforms. Sat. 30th Dec. 1972
Ulsterbus Ltd.   Not transferable: Issued subject to published conditions.
Not authentic unless validated by ticket machine.   **0031**

DE 938
30
PENCE

Number 995 (5995 EZ) was one of the last group of Leyland PD3 double-deckers built by the UTA in 1963. Alongside it, in Bangor in June 1967, No 876 (876 AZ) shows off the former UTA livery and also displays the rear luggage boot, a distinctive feature of this type within the UTA fleet and rarely found on double-deckers elsewhere. *R Whitford*

In later years the blue area above the lower saloon windows of the Leyland PD3 double-deckers was extended downwards. By the time this photo was taken of No 790 (790 EZ) in Magherafelt, vehicles of this type were also one-man operated, usually indicated in the upper destination screen. *I Houston*

Number 900 (900 AZ) was one of a group allocated exclusively by the UTA to Derry city service C (Creggan), the only route in Derry city operated by double-deckers. This arrangement was continued by Ulsterbus until the buses were replaced by modern single-deckers. However, on this occasion, in August 1971, the bus was engaged on a private hire operation along with vehicles from CIÉ and Lough Swilly.   *H Cunningham*

The prototype Leyland Tiger Cub, with Saro body, which had been purchased by the UTA after operating as a Leyland demonstrator was No 301 (PZ 4874). It was later purchased for preservation and restored to its original UTA colours and fleet number 8995 borne as a demonstrator.   *H Cunningham*

Representing the standard production of Leyland Tiger Cubs with bodywork built by the UTA, No 346 (UZ 346) looks very smart as it waits for the start of the first ITT Bus and Coach Rally at Montgomery Road, Belfast, on 29 April 1972.   *H Cunningham*

The second batch of ex-UTA Tiger Cubs is represented here by No 404 (UZ 7404), loading up at Oxford Street bus station before a journey to Ballygowan in September 1972.   *R Bell*

The former demonstrator and prototype Albion Aberdonian with Alexander body, No 60 (TGB 652) pauses on the forecourt of Dromore depot on a snowy day in February 1969. *R Whitford*

An early repaint among the UTA-built Albion Aberdonian fleet was No 63 (1063 XI), parked in Portadown in May 1967. *H Cunningham*

The second batch of vehicles built by the UTA with the style of bodywork derived from the Alexander design was on Leyland Tiger Cub chassis. Number 434 (7434 CZ) is shown in Duncrue Street Yard.

H Cunningham

Number 456 (7456 CZ) started life as a 37-seat luxury coach with the distinctive alloy waist moulding, which affected the application of the Ulsterbus livery. When photographed in June 1967, it displayed the early form of the fleet name.

R Whitford

AEC Reliance chassis were also fitted by the UTA with the same design of bodywork. Number 267 (6267 EZ) was an early repaint with the large fleet-name and was photographed in front of Lisburn station.

H Cunningham

This view of No 235 (6235 EZ), taken in Ballymena several years later, shows the later form of livery, with the waistband picked out in ivory. AECs could usually be distinguished from Albions and Tiger Cubs at a glance by the one-piece windscreen. However, in later years many were modified by fitting of the split windscreen, as shown here.

I Houston

Number 233 (7233 FZ) represents the group of buses built by the UTA specifically for Londonderry city services, and was one of the first to be repainted into Ulsterbus colours. It was photographed alongside the city's former GNR(I) station in May 1967. At that time, the station building continued to house one Ulsterbus engineering clerk who occupied the stationmaster's office.   *R Whitford*

Three of these 20-seaters had been built by the UTA on Austin T200 chassis cowls. Fleet No 1 (8813 AZ) was photographed in Newry in April 1968. I subsequently arranged disposal of this vehicle and of the similar No 3 to Scout groups in Edinburgh.   *H Cunningham*

Six 20-seaters were built by the UTA on Bedford VAS5 chassis in 1963 for lightly loaded rural school transport services. Ulsterbus quickly increased their seating to their design capacity of 28, as shown in this picture of No 5 (15 EZ) leaving Duncrue Street workshops in July 1967. Most of these vehicles worked in the Claudy area of County Londonderry, although one was based in Ballymena for the Buckna route.   *H Cunningham*

This Bedford SB5 with Duple Midland bodywork had been purchased by the UTA as a prototype for a large fleet of school buses built in Duncrue Street workshops. Number 10 (825 EZ) is pictured in Omagh after a journey on service 75 from its base in Dungannon in June 1971.   *R Bell*

Representing the UTA production of school buses on the Bedford SB5 chassis is a 40-seater, No 22 (22 FZ), photographed in Magherafelt in May 1967. Later vehicles had 49 seats, achieved by having seats for three passengers on one side of the gangway.

H Cunningham

Another unique Bedford inherited from the UTA was the 56-seater bus built on a VAL chassis, fleet No 118 (2318 GZ). It is pictured in June 1971 in Omagh where its days were ended in an army 'controlled' explosion. Earlier it had been based at Bangor, where it acquired the nickname 'Torrey Canyon' after the supertanker of that name.

R Bell

The 35 Bedford SB/Duple Bella Vega coaches, assembled by the UTA in 1964, were contracted to a number of the province's leading hotels. With the downturn in incoming tourism after the onset of the Troubles, these coaches were released from their contracts and were transferred to Ulsterbus's own tours and private hire fleet. One of the first was No 173 (2173 MZ) which was re-liveried by the simple expedient of applying Ulsterbus blue over the hotel colour (red). As the plastic filler on the bodyside moulding was also red, this produced an interesting variation, which was enhanced by the use of fine red edging on the fleet name. The photograph was taken in Coleraine in August 1967.   *H Cunningham*

Later repaints, however, applied the standard layout of blue and ivory, and where necessary, replaced the plastic infill with the standard black. By the time this photograph was taken, in Newcastle in July 1974, No 167 (2167 MZ) was engaged in school transport and had been fitted with a full set of service bus seats salvaged from older buses.   *R Whitford*

The six Wolfhound Express coaches, on Leyland Leopard chassis, were the last coaches built by the UTA, in 1965–6. The Ulsterbus livery application initially retained the zigzag flash as an ivory relief, and also retained the word 'Express'. This was perhaps the first application of the 'Ulsterbus Express' branding which was to be given major prominence later. Number 484 (2484 OZ) was photographed in April 1972 during layover on a private hire visiting Bangor.   *R Whitford*

Later in life these vehicles were downgraded to service buses, with a simpler livery and in some cases a change of seating. When photographed in Antrim, No 481 (2481 OZ) had been reseated as a 64-seater for school transport.   *I Houston*

The shorter-length Wolfhound, No 486 (2486 OZ), was the last vehicle to be built by the UTA, in 1966. Appropriately, it was also the last of the former UTA vehicles to be operated in service by Ulsterbus.

I Houston

The 15 Leyland Leopard L1 coaches purchased from Western SMT had been used by the UTA in their original black and white livery, earning them the nickname 'magpies'. No 528 (OCS 728) was photographed on a private hire trip to Bangor in September 1966.

R Whitford

They were quickly recalled by Ulsterbus to Duncrue Street workshops for repainting, removal of toilets and for seating changes. This view outside the workshops in February 1967 shows No 539 (OCS 739) after repainting but before the other work mentioned had been tackled. Most of the vehicles had seating capacity raised from 30 to 36, retaining the original seats, but some were reseated with other seat frames. *R Whitford*

Later in life most of these coaches were reseated again, with service bus seat frames and capacity was raised to 41. This view of Nos 527 and 538 (OCS 727/38), taken in Downpatrick depot, shows the standard service bus seating, and the final, plainer livery.

I Houston

Although purchased in the closing months of the UTA, the batch of 48 Leyland Tiger Cubs obtained from Edinburgh were not placed into service until they had been repainted into Ulsterbus colours. No 9313 (SWS 13) was the first to enter service in the new livery and also the only vehicle to receive the new Ulsterbus logo design, although it was widely used as a woven badge on staff uniforms. The spelling error on this destination display was not unique on the special screens which had to be ordered for these buses, as the standard UTA screens did not fit the narrow aperture. The photograph was taken in Portadown in November 1967.   *H Cunningham*

This later view, taken at Smithfield bus station in October 1970, shows No 1021 (SWS 21) after the renumbering of the batch in 1969. This was one of several of these buses which retained its 'Edinburgh Castle' badge on the front panel.   *R Bell*

New vehicles

The 1967 new arrivals were eagerly awaited, as in most depots these were the first new vehicles for three years. Number 9207 (1207 TZ) is pictured on delivery to Dungannon depot, where Inspector Bob McKeown and driver Billy Irwin were keen to be included in the photograph. *H Cunningham*

Opposite bottom: Although easily identified as a Alexander 'Y'- type design, the bodywork on No 488 (488 TZ) was actually built under licence by Potter of Belfast on Leyland Leopard chassis. The vehicle is depicted in June 1967 outside the Waterside rail station in Londonderry. She was performing a shuttle connection to the city centre, often slotted in between journeys on the long-distance 'Wolfhound Express' services.

R Whitford

Within two years, the entire batch was renumbered as the 1201–70 range and the livery was altered to include a mid-panel band of ivory. The decorative front bumper, which had proved very susceptible to damage, was also removed during overhauls. The value of this modification is well illustrated in this view of No 1245 (1245 TZ) disembarking at Portaferry from the ferry from Strangford during a private hire journey in June 1970.

R Whitford

The similar No 491 (491 TZ) is depicted at Fivemiletown bus park in May 1973, showing the 'Ulsterbus Express' fleet name which had by then replaced the 'Wolfhound' brand inherited from the UTA.　　*R Bell*

First deliveries of new buses for 1968–9 included ten of these semi-coaches on Bristol LH chassis with Potter bodies of a style which was to become the Ulsterbus standard for more than 15 years. Initially, these were used on day tours and private hire and No 1105 (4105 UZ) is seen on the tour departure stand in Glengall Street in June 1969.

H Cunningham

The first batch of Bristol RELLs purchased by Ulsterbus were a specialised design for Londonderry city services. Bodywork, although to Potter of Belfast design, was actually built by Alexander in Falkirk, from whose 'Y' model the Potter design had been derived. The original livery, half ivory and half blue, was the starkest application of the Ulsterbus livery, as shown on No 1052 (9052 UZ) operating along the Spencer Road bus lane in the Waterside in June 1972. *R Bell*

Subsequently, the livery of these buses was brought into line with later additions to the fleet, as shown on No 1059 (9059 UZ) leaving the city centre on a journey to Ballymagroarty. *P Savage*

First of a large fleet of Leyland Leopards, with the typical Ulsterbus bodyshape, were five vehicles specified as express coaches, with high-backed headrest seats. Number 497 (4497 UZ) is depicted when nearly new in Portrush bus station in August 1969. Unlike previous, and later, express coaches, the fleet name on delivery gave no indication of the special function. *R Whitford*

By contrast, No 496 (4496 UZ), pictured in 1976 in Great Victoria Street bus station, has the 'Ulsterbus Express' branding, introduced that year, properly displayed. *R Bell*

The first group of Leyland Leopards with standard 53-seat service bus bodies included No 1314 (4014 WZ), photographed at Ballymena in April 1969.   *R Whitford*

Numbers 1328 and 1329 (4028 WZ and 4029 WZ), two of the 49-seat semi-luxury batch, were pictured in Dublin during a school private hire journey in 1972.   *R Bell*

Number 1337 (4037 WZ) was photographed between journeys in Coleraine depot in 1985, by which time a set of service bus seats had been fitted. This vehicle was later purchased for preservation by the Irish Transport Trust, and its original seating restored. However, it was subsequently destroyed in an arson attack while parked at an Ulsterbus depot. *P Savage*

Number 1345 (AOI 1345) was one of ten buses purchased in 1969, primarily for the airport service. When photographed in 1979, however, it was engaged in the huge private hire operation in connection with the Papal visit to Ireland, which involved more than 700 vehicles travelling to five venues. The 1969 deliveries were the last Leyland Leopards to be supplied with the traditional 'big cat' badge, first introduced on Royal Tigers in 1950, but replaced on this vehicle by the time the picture was taken. *I Houston*

Number 1412 (BOI 1412), new in 1971, heads for Donaghadee from Bangor on service 3, with a large load of passengers in July 1983. *P Savage*

Many Leyland Leopard chassis were refurbished and rebodied after their original bodywork was destroyed in bomb or arson incidents. Number 1398 (BOI 1398), new in 1971 and rebodied in 1973, waits at a picturesque location in the village of Dromara, County Down, terminal on service 26, in 1986. *P Savage*

Number 1441 (COI 1441), another 1973 rebuild, arrives in Ballygowan from Belfast on service 12, early in 1987. *P Savage*

Number 1373 (BOI 1373), which was first registered in 1971, and rebuilt 1973, had reached Banbridge on service 38 from Belfast to Newry when photographed in 1986. This vehicle, with 1380, were given non-standard front panels, based on the style then being fitted to new Bristol LH buses. *P Savage*

Leyland Leopard express coach No 503 (BOI 1503) was in pristine condition at Magherafelt depot in August 1970, soon after delivery to its Dugannon base. *H Cunningham*

One of the 1971 delivery of luxury touring coaches, Plaxton Panorama Elite-bodied No 583 (COI 583) had been relegated to local service duties when photographed in Antrim bus station in 1982. *I Houston*

Also in pristine condition as it arrives from Alexander Coachbuilders in June 1971, No 912 (COI 912) was one of the first two completed of 40 double-deckers on Leyland Atlantean chassis ordered by Ulsterbus. Detail changes were made to later vehicles, including the fitting of heavy galvanised steel side bumpers and a change to the front panel above the destination screen to permit the display of advertisements.

H Cunningham

Opposite bottom : In later years double-deckers were concentrated in rural areas to cope with heavy demand for school transport. This line-up in Omagh in 1983 includes three of the original Ulsterbus Atlanteans, together with four of the shorter Atlanteans purchased second-hand from Strathclyde PTE.

R Bell

After the first dozen Leyland Atlanteans were built in 1971, there was a lengthy gap before the construction of double-deckers resumed. One of the first of the second group to arrive was No 927 (COI 927), shown participating in the first ITT Bus and Coach Rally at Luke's Point, Bangor in April 1972. Driver (later Inspector) Billy Redpath of Smithfield depot was in the hot seat before the manoeuvring tests. *H Cunningham*

Bristol LH6L, No 1640 (FOI 1640) displays the predominantly ivory livery introduced on new buses in 1973, before setting off from Montgomery Road on the 1973 Bus and Coach Rally. This vehicle, together with No 1629, were the first of the type to enter service. *H Cunningham*

Later in life these buses reverted to the standard livery, with additional areas of blue across the front panel and down to the skirts at the sides. This is illustrated on No 1659 (FOI 1659), photographed in 1979 approaching Foyle Street bus station, Derry, to take up service. *R Bell*

The Bedford YRQ and YRT types, delivered in 1974, also carried the predominantly ivory livery. Although intended for operation on rural services, No 1798 (HOI 1798) was photographed displaying a town service destination in Bangor depot in October 1974, before entering service.

R Whitford

Outstations often had a full allocation of these rural buses. Three Bedford YRQs were in residence in Carnlough when photographed in 1977. All had reverted to the standard fleet livery. Nearest the camera are Nos 1790 and 1753 (HOI 1790 and HOI 1753), both of which were later converted into engineering department towing vehicles.

R Bell

Although Ulsterbus purchased 25 of the longer version of the Bedford chassis, bearing the model designation YRT, these proved less successful in service and were withdrawn earlier. First of the batch, No 1801 (GOI 1801) is seen in Bangor in 1980 after a lengthy private hire run from its base in Newry.   *R Bell*

Several of the YLQ type were based at Rathfriland, where No 1877 (LOI 1877) is seen preparing to depart for Newcastle on service 36.   *P Savage*

Although purchased in 1975 as an express coach, by 1980, when this photograph was taken at Stoneyford, Leyland Leopard No 1905 (HOI 1905) was working local services and not displaying an 'Express' branding.

R Bell

Number 1926 (HOI 1926), one of the 1975 semi-luxury batch of Leyland Leopards, looks fresh and new when photographed in Bangor depot in January 1975. Although outwardly identical to the express group, these vehicles had the less versatile four-speed gearbox.

R Whitford

From 1976, Ulsterbus standardised on the five-speed gearbox on its Leyland Leopard semi-luxury coaches, making them capable performers on a wide range of services and private hire journeys. Number 1948 (KOI 9946) was pictured in 1985 performing local service work. After the destruction of Smithfield bus station, services to the north of Belfast departed from Laganbank Road, adjacent to Oxford Street bus station.

P Savage

Opposite bottom: Representing the 1978 deliveries, No 108 (ROI 108) is pictured very soon after entering service at the Larne harbour passenger terminal while working the Northern Ireland portion of the Cross Channel Express service. Unusually, this batch was released with both the 'Ulsterbus Express' branding and the standard Ulsterbus fleet name and logo.

K Thomson

Number 1979 (NOI 1979) of the 1977 delivery is shown working the cross-border express service 270, leaving Cavan. Ironically, after its 15 years' service, this vehicle passed to Bus Éireann for further service.

K Thomson

Four Leyland Leopard coaches with Duple Dominant I bodies had been bought in 1978, primarily for express services, and six similar vehicles followed in 1979. Number 102 (ROI 102) is seen at Foyle Street bus station, Londonderry, before a departure to Belfast in 1983.   *P Savage*

Later in life several of these coaches were painted in this yellow and black livery and dedicated to the Airbus service to and from Aldergrove Airport. Number 155 (TOI 155) pauses to set down a passenger in Glengall Street in June 1984. A misguided attempt was made to rename the world-famous Europa Hotel as the Forum Hotel, but it soon reverted to its original appellation.   *R Bell*

Leyland Leopard No 135 (ROI 135), new in 1978, is pictured in 1980 at the suburban Rosevale Park terminus, outside Belfast. *R Bell*

Number 186 (VOI 186), delivered in 1980, is pictured in 1986 in Bushmills on service 132 from Ballymoney. *P Savage*

Number 241 (WOI 2241), which was delivered in 1981, was spotted the same year in Bangor during a major private hire operation. *R Bell*

Although most of the Leyland Leopards had been specified as 49-seat semi-coaches, a few batches in the latter years of production were ordered as 53-seat service buses. One such was No 292 (AXI 292), delivered in 1982 and pictured in 1988 during layover at the Mall, Armagh. *I Houston*

The last deliveries of Leyland Leopards took place in 1983. One of these, No 335 (BXI 335), is seen departing from Glengall Street on the infrequent service 106 to Leathemstown. *P Savage*

During 1981 two Leyland Leopard chassis were allocated to Wright of Ballymena to enable them to complete two prototype vehicles to full PSV specification. Number 258 (XOI 2258) was delivered in the early summer of 1982 as a semi-luxury vehicle, and is pictured two years later at Dublin Airport, working the seasonal service then established from and to Belfast. It was also the regular performer on the Belfast–Larne Harbour connections for the cross-channel express services, hence the 'London Ulsterman' branding. *R Bell*

The second Wright vehicle was specified as a luxury coach for express services and private hire. The photograph, taken in Carnlough, shows the vehicle in its original livery, working service 252, the Antrim Coast Express. It has recently been acquired for preservation by the Irish Transport Trust and is to be restored to this original livery. *P Savage*

Although purchased as an express coach, No 558 (WOI 2258) was retained by the Tours department for several summers, and is seen here at Stranmillis Embankment during a school private hire. *R Bell*

When deliveries of Bristol RELLs with Gardner engines commenced in 1975, two batches with centre doors were taken for urban services in Londonderry, Craigavon and Newtownabbey, but most of these were later concentrated in Derry. Number 2003 (JOI 2003) of the first group is seen at Altnagelvin Hospital. This was of several vehicles with experimental rubber corners added to the steel bumpers. *I Houston*

Number 2131 (MOI 2131), of the group delivered in 1976–7 for operation in Newtownabbey, and later transferred to Londonderry, departs Guildhall Square, the traditional terminus of the city services, to operate the service to Nelson Drive, in 1980. Since then the Square has been pedestrianised, and bus departures moved to Foyle Street. *R Bell*

Number 2133 (MOI 2133) of the same group, new in 1977, climbs steep Shipquay Street from Shipquay Gate, illustrating two features which powerfully influenced the specification for city service buses in the 'Maiden City'.
P Savage

Opposite bottom: Number 2286 (TOI 2286), new in 1979, passes the Adair Arms Hotel in 1981, while working the Ballymena town service 124. This route was typical of the suburban services for which the Bristol RELLs were ideally suited.

R Bell

Single-door Bristol RELLs became by far the most numerous type and proved suitable for a wide range of local bus duties. Number 2374 (UOI 2374) of the 1980 delivery is shown in a rear end pose in Great Victoria Street depot, to illustrate the distinctive rear end treatment specified on all Bristol RELLs for Ulsterbus and Citybus. The centre rear emergency door improved access to the rear for cleaning and, in the absence of a luggage boot, for occasional loading of luggage or parcels. It also permitted a low window aperture, which assisted drivers' vision to the rear when reversing, and doubled the number of potential advertising spaces.

Author

Number 2434 (WOI 2434) arrives in Royal Avenue, Belfast city centre, on service 163 from Carrickfergus in 1982. 'Skybreaker' panels were fitted to large numbers of the later Bristol RELLs to increase revenue from commercial advertising.　　　　　　　　　　　　　　　　　　　　　　　　　　　　　　　　　*R Bell*

Number 2592 (BXI 2592) of 1983, one of the last group to be delivered, prepares to leave Bangor bus and rail station on the town service to Kilmaine in the same year.　　　　　　　　　　　　　　　　　　*R Bell*

The prototype Leyland B21 had a centre exit Alexander body. After extensive pave testing, this vehicle reached Ulsterbus in 1982 as No 3000 (WOI 607). It spent most of its service life on the Larne town service 159 to and from Antiville from Larne depot, where it was photographed in 1984. *R Bell*

Early in 1982, five of the B21s purchased by Ulsterbus and Citybus were driven round the province in convoy to conduct fuel consumption comparisons. Before departure the vehicles were prepared at Great Victoria Street depot, where No 3001 (WOI 3001) was photographed alongside No 3000 (WOI 607). Behind these was Gardner-engined No 3005 (WOI 3005) which achieved the lowest fuel consumption. Inside 3001 are Maurice Kennedy and myself (driver's seat). *R Bell*

The first Leyland Tiger with the newly designed Alexander 'N'-type body to be completed, in January 1984, was No 340 (DXI 3340) which is seen in Oxford Street bus station, operating the service 20 to Newcastle and Kilkeel. The new style of Ulsterbus fleet name adopted was then the standard lettering style for publicity, but was deemed less effective on this application and replaced on later deliveries by a more forceful, upper case style of block lettering. The livery also had been updated, showing a greater area of blue on the upper part of the body compared to previous deliveries.   *P Savage*

Leyland Tiger No 398 (FXI 398) was 'snapped' in September 1984 at Crumlin Primary School, close to the bridge carrying the Antrim–Lisburn railway branch line over the village. These vehicles were almost better known throughout the fleet as the 'Turbos' rather than as the 'Tigers'.   *R Bell*

In each of the years 1984, 1986 and 1988, ten of the Tigers were delivered with a version of the 'N'- type body specially upgraded for express service work. The angled windows at the front and rear of the saloon (actually glasses from the rear windows of Bristol RELLs) allowed a bold blue stripe to be applied to the bodyside, upswept at the front, also incorporating a larger version of the by then familiar 'Ulsterbus Express' branding. Number 365 (DXI 3365) of the 1984 group is shown loading outside the Bus Éireann office in Cavan town, before departing for Belfast on the Interlink Ireland service 271.   *R Bell*

Number 469 (HXI 469) of the second (1986) tranche of express Tigers was photographed in 1987 outside Larne Harbour passenger terminal, awaiting passengers from the cross-channel ferry connection.   *R Bell*

Number 429 (GXI 429), new in 1985, was photographed in 1987 crossing a Bailey bridge near Killymaddy on the main Dungannon to Ballygawley road, while working service 78 to Omagh.   *P Savage*

Introducing a new numbering series, No 1001 (IXI 1001) was photographed on arrival at Bangor depot after delivery in September 1986.   *R Whitford*

Late in 1988, as a stopgap arrangement in the absence of an ideal city service design, a group of ten Leyland Tigers were specified for Derry city services. Four single seats and a pram pen gave more space for passenger circulation in the gangway. This marked the first use of the Tiger model as a replacement for the Bristol RELL on its typical territory. Number 1208 (NXI 1208) is seen in Foyle Street working to Slievemore while still very new. *P Savage*

Ulsterbus received only two of the 1986 trial batch of Leyland Lynx chassis with Alexander 'N'-type bodies. both were operated from Lisburn, where 3012 (HXI 3012) is seen. Both vehicles were transferred to Citybus in 1989 and the entire batch was sold to Stevensons of Uttoxeter a few years later. *R Bell*

Second-hand vehicles

The first second-hand acquisition after Ulsterbus was formed was a Leyland Tiger Cub with Alexander body. This was acquired from 6th Newtownards Scouts, but had started its life with Edinburgh Corporation. It is seen taking on passengers in Portrush bus station in May 1972. The driver is much more interested in the photographer than his passengers! There must be some doubt as to the authenticity of the Cushendall destination display, as the vehicle was based in Magherafelt. *H Cunningham*

When Coastal Bus Service was acquired in April 1974, few of their vehicles were regarded as having a long-term place in the Ulsterbus fleet. Number 229 (327 NMP), an AEC Reliance and originally a manufacturer's demonstrator, was operated in the Ballymena area for four years. She was repainted in 1975 and photographed in October 1977. *R Whitford*

Also from the Coastal Bus Service fleet, this Leyland Leopard with Duple Commodore bodywork was No 500 (AWT 295B) and was overhauled and repainted for service in the Coleraine area. The photograph suggests that the coach had been reseated with seats from a former UTA Albion or Tiger Cub coach. The vehicle was subsequently sold for further service to Lough Swilly in 1976. *R Bell*

Although Coastal Bus Service had assembled a fleet of six Bedford VAL14 coaches, all with Duple Vega Major bodies, these were not favoured by Ulsterbus, and none were repainted. Number 1271 (CTD 324B) was used on coaching duties until the end of 1974 and is seen in central Belfast during the summer of that year.

I Houston

AEC Merlins from London Transport, Nos 2518 (VLW 387G) and 2494 (VLW 527G), are seen here in Pennyburn depot, Londonderry, in 1978. The former, acquired in 1977, has had its lower panels repainted in a darker shade of red. The latter had previously been operated by Citybus.   *H Cunningham*

Numbers 2522 (VLW 366G) and 2519 (AML 651H) were two of the Merlins which received full Ulsterbus livery and are depicted in Newry depot ready for service. Both gave three years of service.   *I Houston*

The shorter AECs acquired from London Transport, known by them as Swifts, proved very unreliable and none were kept in service for more than two years. The example seen here in Oxford Street depot, after the destruction of Smithfield, had been prepared for service by Citybus, hence the large fleet numbers. Number 12 (EGN 559J) gave only two months' service, although it survived for many years as a store for engineering material at Lisburn.   *I Houston*

The first purchase of second-hand Leyland Leopards comprised seven with Plaxton coach bodies acquired from Grey Green of London in 1978. Whilst a few were retained by the Tours department, most were used on express services. Number 572 (EMD 610J) is seen leaving Glengall Street in 1979, with a substantial load of passengers bound for Enniskillen.   *R Bell*

Some of the Leyland Leopards acquired from Southdown in 1979 were pressed into service in their original owner's green livery. Number 1192 (HUF 768E) is seen in Ballymoney depot shortly after entering service.

R Bell

Although acquired from Southdown, three of the batch arrived in red livery, having already been loaned to Alder Valley. Number 1187 (EUF 141D) was the first of the batch and entered service in Dungannon in April 1979.

R Bell

Others were fully repainted into Ulsterbus colours. Number 1168 (HUF 766E) was photographed at Ravenhill during a major private hire operation for the rugby Schools' Cup Final in 1980.   *R Bell*

Ten of these coach-seated Leyland Leopards were purchased from Ribble Motor Services in 1979. Number 1145 (CRN 824D) is seen in Laganbank Road between journeys to and from Newtownabbey.

R Bell

A further batch of short Leyland Leopards purchased from Ribble in 1980 started to enter service the following year. Most saw little service, but No 1131 (DRN 667D), seen here in Foyle Street in 1984, gave almost three years' service on Derry city services and had been fully repainted in a darker shade of red. The grey stripe was reminiscent of the ex-London Merlins. *R Bell*

This 12 m Leyland Leopard with Plaxton Panorama Elite coachwork with Duple seats had been pride of the fleet at Grey Green coaches of London. It was one of four 12-m-long 57-seaters acquired by Ulsterbus for the touring fleet in 1980, and was photographed in Great Victoria Street on arrival from Duncrue Street workshops. Apparently the destination display was inherited from Grey Green! *R Bell*

Although widely used by Citybus, only limited numbers of the second-hand Bristol REs were allocated to Ulsterbus, mainly to Derry city services. Number 765 (OWY 749K), an RESL ex-West Yorkshire, enters Foyle Street bus station in 1984. Inspector Ernie Crown seems more concerned with watching the photographer.

R Bell

Second-hand Bristol RELL, No 795 (WNO 539L), an ex-Eastern National, loads passengers for the Creggan service at Guildhall Square, below the historic city walls in 1986. Use of the route number screens to display the fleet number is a trait more associated with Lough Swilly buses. *R Bell*

Three Leyland Atlanteans, dating from 1967, from the Citybus fleet passed to Ulsterbus in 1977, but gave little service. Number 2706 (1706 MZ) was photographed in Pennyburn depot, and retained its red livery.

K Thomson

These were followed by fourteen Daimler Fleetline double-deckers with Potter bodies, most of which were repainted blue and gave two to three years' service. Number 2712 (712 UZ) was transferred in January 1978 and served until 1982. It is seen loading passengers in Portrush bus station, with the distinctive mock Tudor tower of the railway station in the background.

I Houston

One Fleetline which lasted very much longer was Number 2716 (716UZ), which had already been rebodied with an Alexander (Belfast) body designed to resemble the earlier style of Belfast Corporation Daimler Fleetlines. This vehicle is shown in Ulsterbus colours in Portrush bus station in 1978. It was selected to become the first Ulsterbus open-top double-decker in 1981.

R Bell

Four of these Leyland Atlanteans were purchased from British Airways (originally British Overseas Airways Corporation) and refitted as 69-seater service buses. Number 954 (LYF 318D) is seen in Omagh depot in June 1979.

R Bell

This was one of 25 double-deck Leyland Atlanteans purchased from Strathclyde PTE. Number 956 (MDS 669 P) was photographed in Portrush in August 1982. This vehicle gave 10 years of service, although this was exceptional.

R Whitford

One of the former Lothian Leyland Atlanteans was photographed in virtually the same location about five years later. Number 900 (WFS 290K) saw service from 1986 until 1991.

R Bell

Sureline's fleet, acquired in 1987, was largely composed of former Ulsterbus vehicles. None of the eight Bristol LHs were retained in service, but of the 13 Leyland Leopards, nine remained in service temporarily until more modern replacements could be drafted in; the last were withdrawn after eight months. A group of these Leopards is shown in Craigavon depot shortly after the transfer. Nearest the camera, No 671 (4011 WZ), previously fleet No 1311, was used for seven months.

I Houston

The Sureline trading name and livery was retained for some time in the Craigavon area, where this 1979 Ford R1114 coach, No 696 (FIB 8279), with Duple Dominant II body, was operating when photographed in 1987.

R Bell

Opposite top: This former Sureline Ford/Plaxton Supreme coach, No 695 (FIB 4533), dating from 1980, migrated as far as Londonderry, where this unique version of the Ulsterbus coaching livery was applied. The photograph was taken in 1989.

I Houston

Opposite bottom: The flagship of the Sureline Coaches fleet had been this DAF MB200 with Plaxton Viewmaster bodywork. It was taken into the Ulsterbus Tours fleet and given a very hurried livery change after acquisition of that business in June 1987. Number 697 (HIB 9482) is seen here in the coach park at Glenveigh National Park, County Donegal, dominated by the distinctive shape of Muckish Mountain.

Author

Minibuses

During the 1984–5 period the bus industry nationally became very interested in the use of small buses, based on commercial vans. In many places, small coach operators had demonstrated that a useful and viable niche market could be developed for the use of such vehicles on a private hire or contract hire basis. With the looming prospect of deregulation in the industry, the larger operators were considering the part which small buses and high frequencies could play in either a defensive or a predatory role in the operation of competing services. A lead was taken, on behalf of the NBC group, by Devon General in Exeter, where the growth of passenger numbers achieved by high frequencies was spectacular and the pattern was soon taken up by other operators in the run up to deregulation in 1986.

Although deregulation of bus services in Northern Ireland was not an early option, Ulsterbus management recognised the potential niche market which could be developed in the private hire field, and that such vehicles could also be used to develop new and innovative services which would stand little chance of viability for full-size bus and coach operation. This resulted in the formation of Flexibus Limited (using the existing legal framework of Coastal Bus Services Ltd, which had been retained as a dormant subsidiary since 1974). The first vehicle was a Mercedes 608D/Reeves Burgess conversion, which was used to launch a new service between Belfast city centre and the rapidly developing Belfast Harbour Airport. This vehicle was followed by two more Mercedes 608Ds with PMT conversions. Potteries Motor Traction was one of the NBC companies which had established a successful subsidiary operating small coaches, which the management team responsible for Flexibus had visited. The initial range of varied size vehicles was completed with one Mercedes 207D, one Talbot Express and one Renault Traffic Master, all with conversions by Wright of Ballymena. From this point on Ulsterbus's own Central Workshops established a new-build programme, which continued to convert Mercedes 608D vans but including two more Renault Traffic Masters and four Iveco 60.10V vans during a shortage of Mercedes vehicles. Production then switched to the Mercedes 609D model, introduced during 1986. By this time Flexibus operations were being rolled out from Belfast to the provincial depots.

By 1987, the decision had been taken to move into small bus operation on more conventional local bus routes, particularly in the provincial towns. The new type of local bus service was first launched in Bangor, late in 1987, with four Mercedes 609D vehicles. A further 18 similar vehicles were introduced during 1988, when also the brand name for the new mode of operation – 'Busybus' – was decided upon, and a more striking livery introduced. Four MCW 'Metrorider' vehicles were purchased to convert the Airbus service to the new form of operation. The continued expansion of this type of operation will be documented in a later volume.

The first Flexibus vehicle was fleet No 1 (DXI 9001), a Mercedes 608D/Reebur conversion, initially used to launch a regular service between Belfast city centre and Belfast Harbour Airport. Photographs for publicity purposes were taken in 1984 on the airside, alongside a DHC Twin Otter of Spacegrand (forerunner of Jersey European).

Author

This early Flexibus publicity photograph, taken at Belvoir Forest car park, shows the full range of vehicles offered by 1986, ranging from the 19-seat Mercedes 608Ds through the 13-seat Renault Traffic Masters to the 12-seat Mercedes 207D.

Ulsterbus

Flexibus operations were by no means confined to Northern Ireland. Here Mercedes 608D No 7 (HXI 4007) is seen at Sumburgh Head in the Shetland Islands. In front of the coach are Fred Buick, Ulsterbus depot manager, Londonderry, and Max Hale, Area Manager, Belfast, for Ulsterbus and Citybus.

Author

The Mercedes 609D van was adopted as the base vehicle for minicoach conversion in the company's own workshops as soon as it became available in 1986. Fleet No 28 (KXI 1028) of the 1987 production was posed for publicity photographs in Belvoir Forest Park. Driver Lynn Watson extends an invitation to board.

Ulsterbus

Although this new Mercedes 609D/Wright conversion had been delivered to Sureline, it had not entered service by the handover date. It duly entered service as Flexibus No 31 (CDZ 6664), although retained in Craigavon and in Sureline colours.

I Houston

Urban minibus services started modestly with four minibuses on Bangor town services in September 1987. On the first day of operation, No 801 (KXI 7801), a Mercedes 609D converted in Ulsterbus's own workshops, is seen in Balloo estate in the rather bland original livery. At this stage Ulsterbus managers were still debating a catchy brand name.

P Savage

A year later, the Busybus name and logo (designed by myself) were adopted, with a more striking livery of blue, ivory and yellow stripes as shown on No 818 (NXI 818) in service in Regent Street, Newtownards.

P Savage

Minibus operation was also adopted for the Airbus service between Belfast and Aldergrove Airport in 1988. One of the MCW Metroriders bought for this service is seen in the new blue, white and green livery requested by the airport, on stand 1 of Glengall Street bus station.

P Savage

Demonstrators

Ulsterbus gave serious consideration in 1967 to purchasing used buses from Stockholm, Sweden, rendered surplus by their impending change to driving on the left. This Scania Vabis was supplied on test, was registered 920TZ in Northern Ireland and was photographed in March 1967 on Derry city service G to Clooney, passing the distinctive Pennyburn Chapel. The vehicle proved most unsuitable, the weight of the American designed bus resulting in a fuel consumption almost twice that of the contemporary AEC Reliance city buses.

R Whitford

Bus manufacturers provide demonstration vehicles in the hope that operators will be persuaded to place orders. Perhaps the most successful ever was this Bristol RELL, tried on Derry city services late in 1967, resulting in Ulsterbus and Citybus eventually purchasing 620 new vehicles of the type. LAE 770E emerges from Buncrana Road on service G to Clooney.

H Cunningham

AEC Swift LYY 827D, tested in direct comparison with the Bristol RELL, emerges from Altnagelvin Hospital en route to Rosemount. After a varied career, the vehicle was later acquired by Ulsterbus with the Coastal Bus business in 1974.   *R Whitford*

Mercedes were trying to become established in the British market in 1969, and in March of that year provided this O302 model coach VMK 275G for trials on the airport service.   *R Whitford*

During 1970, when MCW were launching their Metro-Scania into the market, their demonstrator VWD 451H was operated in various depots and also performed a fuel consumption test run round the province. It is seen here in July 1970, loading passengers in Glengall Street for an express journey to Newry.   *R Bell*

Bedford YRQ with Willowbrook body, EXE 276J, temporary Ulsterbus fleet No.2, arrives in Donaghadee on a journey from Bangor in August 1971.   *R Whitford*

Ford R192, CNO 797G, also with Willowbrook body, came as a demonstrator late in 1970 and was purchased by Ulsterbus as fleet No 1100 the following year. It is seen leaving Glengall Street on a journey to Londonderry. *R Bell*

Ford displayed this R192/ Willowbrook vehicle in full Ulsterbus livery at the Earl's Court Motor Show in 1970. KEV 953J later operated in Lisburn as fleet No 3 during late 1971/early 1972. Engineering Manager Billy Woods is standing inside the bus. *Author*

In April 1972, Seddon provided this Pennine IV (KWW 901K) for trials; it is seen here in Bangor.

R Whitford

Leyland National EOI 8060 arrived as a demonstrator with the Workington factory's closest 'standard livery' to that of Ulsterbus. It carried the temporary fleet number 3 when photographed on Bangor town service in November 1972.

R Whitford

Later, after purchase of the vehicle by Ulsterbus in 1973, it was renumbered 1600 and the livery brought closer to Ulsterbus standards. It was used almost exclusively on the Larne town service to and from Antiville estate, and this destination was a permanent display for many years. This could be misleading on the rare occasions when the vehicle was on private hire, as in this photograph at Mossley. Driver Alan Cahoon of Larne was in charge.

I Houston

Not strictly a demonstrator, this Karrier school bus, owned by the Western Education and Library Board, was borrowed in 1980 and fitted out for full PSV operation to maintain the public bus service between Coleraine and Limavady, via Downhill, during roadworks which imposed a severe weight limitation. BJI 1372 was given the temporary fleet No 1372.

R Bell

This Leyland Tiger/Plaxton Elite demonstration coach, FRN 801W, was tried out on the cross-channel express services from Stranraer during 1981.

Author

Optare offered this 'Starrider' on Mercedes chassis for demonstration during 1988. E456 VUM was photographed at Bladnoch on the Scottish 'Macharsbus' service operated by Ulsterbus that year. The vehicle was also tried out on the Airbus service and on the Omagh–Longford Interlink service.

Author

Touring coaches

Three pairs of AEC Reliances with Plaxton coachwork had been introduced by the UTA between 1960 and 1964. Initially Ulsterbus intended that the existing livery of two shades of blue would be retained on these coaches for the luxury tours business, which was to operate under a new 'Ulster Coach Tours' brand name. However, the livery plan was changed in 1968 and the six 'Plaxtons' were turned out in ivory and blue. Number 590 (1015 AZ) shows this livery with both Ulsterbus Ltd and Ulster Coach Tours fleet names on the rear, as it leaves the central workshops in April 1968.

R Whitford

One of the former UTA AEC Reliance/Plaxton Panorama touring coaches, No 594 (494 EZ), was specially prepared to launch the company's new Grand Highland Tour of Scotland and is seen here on a driver familiarisation tour in April 1968, disembarking the Erskine Ferry over the River Clyde, later replaced by the high level Erskine Bridge.

Author

This line of Ulster Coach Tours vehicles was photographed in April 1967. It includes five of the six new Leyland Leopard coaches with Plaxton Panorama bodies delivered in 1967, together with all six of the Plaxton-bodied AEC Reliances inherited from the UTA. *R Whitford*

Although the vehicles concerned had not been repainted, artistic licence was used to represent the new livery, in the style applied to the AEC Plaxtons, for the 1969 season brochure. The same illustration headed colourful posters which were used by the publicity department for many years. *Ulsterbus*

However, this livery was never applied to the 1967 Plaxtons. When they were repainted, the style adopted was more like the bus fleet, with more blue than ivory below the waist, as shown on No 587 (587 TZ) at Stranraer harbour in June 1971. *Author*

Six Leyland Leopard coaches with Plaxton Elite bodywork were purchased in 1971 for extended tours work, mainly at that time in Scotland and England. Driver Bobby Herron collects passengers for No 582 (COI 582) at the Cairnryan Hotel. *Author*

After experimenting with a hired 29-seater coach, Ulsterbus Tours purchased this Bedford VAS with Duple Bella Vista body in 1973. Number 577 (HOI 577) was used on tours to remote areas of the Scottish Highlands and Islands, and for small private hire groups. It is seen here in Glencoe, dwarfed hy the bulk of Buachaille Etive Mor. *Author*

1974 marked the change from Plaxton to Duple coachwork, with the adoption of their new 'Dominant' model, on two Bedford YRQ and two Leyland Leopard chassis. Two further Leylands were added later in the year. One of these, Leyland Leopard coach No 1909 (HOI 1909), is seen resting at Larne Harbour after a connection from Belfast with Cross Channel Express passengers bound for Blackpool. *M Collins*

Later in life these coaches were relegated to local express services and the airport service. However, No 1912 (HOI 1912) was on a special assignment when it was spotted outside the great Palm House, designed by Charles Lanyon, in Belfast's Botanic Gardens in 1985.

P Savage

Two more Bedfords, with YLQ chassis and Duple Dominant bodies, were added to the fleet in 1976 as Nos 1831 and 1832 (LOI 1831 and LOI 1832). These later became 'Executive Club Coaches' with fewer seats grouped around tables, as shown in this view posed on the Annadale Embankment.

R Bell

An opportunity to update the smallest type of coach in the tours fleet arose when Ulsterbus acquired another Bedford VAS5 from Weatherdair of Ballywalter, who had used it for staff transport. The more modern Duple 'Baby Dominant' body on this coach matched the larger vehicles in the fleet. The vehicle provided the connection from and to Belfast on the occasion of the first arrival in June 1978 of Western Ferries' catamaran *Highland Seabird* on its new service from Oban, in Argyll, to Portrush.   *Author*

Six new coaches for the 1977 season were Leyland Leopards with Duple Dominant II bodies. Number 1990 (NOI 1990) is seen near Nuremberg, West Germany, during a staff tour in 1977. Werner Heubeck is deep in conversation with Citybus driver Andy Montgomery, while Billy Campbell, the MD's chauffeur, watches the camera.   *Author*

Four identical vehicles were added to the coach fleet in 1979. One of these, No 1997 (TOI 1997), is seen amidst the grandeur of the English Lake District at Ambleside the following year. *Author*

In 1983, two of these Leyland Tigers with Duple Dominant IV coachwork were purchased from dealers' stock, primarily for the cross-channel express services. Number 555 (CXI 1555) is seen outside Stranraer garage prior to departing on the overnight service to Bristol. *Author*

Plaxton secured the 1981 order for new coach bodies, and four Leyland Leopards were built for each of the tours and express fleets. Two of the touring coaches had new features, including steps folding out below the offside emergency door, for operation into continental Europe. Here No 564 (XOI 564) stops under an ancient water tower on the Hunsruck High Road, between the Rhine and Moselle rivers.

Author

The four new coaches for the touring fleet in 1983 marked a major advance in specification. These were on Leyland Tiger chassis with the new Duple Caribbean bodies and were extensively equipped for continental touring. Number 551 (BXI 5551) was photographed in the village of Bacharach on the west bank of the Rhine in June 1984.

Author

The following year saw the addition to the fleet of four Leyland Tigers with the new Wright Contour bodies, the first to be built on 12 m heavyweight chassis. Number 544 (EXI 5544) was posed for publicity photographs at Donaghadee harbour shortly after entering service. *P Savage*

In the same year, four Leyland Tigers with Duple Laser bodies were added to the tours fleet, in the 11 m size, by then regarded as the short length, more suitable for the Highlands of Scotland. Number 546 (EXI 5546) was photographed outside its Stranraer base a year later. *R Bell*

The year 1985 saw the acquisition of four new coaches, all Leyland Tigers, but with three different body specifications. The only Duple was a 12 m Laser II, No 539 (GXI 539), which is pictured at Threave Gardens in Galloway in 1989. *Author*

In 1985, Ulsterbus had a further need for smaller coaches to replace the Bedfords as 'Executive Club Coaches'. Two of the rare 10-m-long Leyland Leopards with Plaxton Supreme bodies were purchased. These had originated with Glenton of London, but were purchased from Craigg of Amble and Procter of Stoke-on-Trent. Number 565 (AJD 165T), which had power doors, is seen in 1987 passing Bladnoch Distillery on its first day of operation on the Macharsbus service between Whithorn and Newton Stewart in Galloway. This was Ulsterbus's only foray into operation of local buses in Scotland and gave the company first-hand experience of the procedures following deregulation of local bus services in Great Britain in 1986. *Author*

In 1986 one Volvo B9M with 10 m, 39-seat Plaxton Panorama body was purchased, initially for a contract which Ulsterbus had secured to operate an Irish tour on behalf of NLM, the Dutch domestic airline. Number 600 (KXI 600) was photographed in Dublin the following year. *R Bell*

The only full size coach added to the tours fleet in 1986 was this Leyland Tiger with Duple 320 55-seat body. Number 536 (IXI 1536) was photographed outside the company's Stranraer garage. *Author*

In 1987, two Duple 340 bodies were purchased, on Leyland Tiger chassis. A unique feature was that the offside continental door was additional to the standard emergency exit at the rear. This allowed the stepwell leading to the continental door to be closed off and four additional seats fitted, increasing the maximum capacity from 53 to 57. The photograph shows No 535 (JXI 535) preparing to leave North Sea Ferries' terminal at Hull after a tour of the Dutch bulbfields in June 1987. Since 1977, the North Sea Ferries (later P&O North Sea Ferries) crossings from Hull have remained the preferred route for most Ulsterbus Tours to and from Continental Europe.

Author

Driver training

Leyland Tiger PS1 8578 (GZ 7646) was retained for driver training duty in Londonderry. It is seen in May 1969 in the temporary yard off Foyle Street established for vehicle cleaning and fuelling.   *R Whitford*

Training duties gave an extended life to several Leyland PD2/10Cs. Here No 682 (UZ 682) takes part in the first Irish Transport Trust Bus and Coach Rally, in April 1972.   *R Bell*

In due course, Leyland Titan PD3s also gave sterling service in the driving school, notably No 824 (8824 AZ) which served from 1975 until 1983 and is pictured on the Malone Road in 1978. An 'all types' PSV driving licence would be issued if the driving test was passed on a double-decker with a manual gearbox. Otherwise the trainee had to be presented for a second test in a different vehicle. The Leyland PD3 was the last model available in the Ulsterbus fleet which met this specification. The additional off-side window for the instructor, whose seat behind the cab was accommodated by removal of the staircase, can be clearly seen, as can the additional rear view mirrors provided for the instructor. This was the only Leyland PD3 to have the livery revised with the all blue driving cab, which was a feature of the Leyland Atlanteans.

R Bell

Opposite bottom: Number 1687 (FOI 1687) is carrying a substantial load of passengers through Glengormley en route to Ballyclare when photographed in 1988, shortly before withdrawal. It was also used for driver training at that time, and brackets fitted to the front panel provided for the display of 'L' plates.

P Savage

When the supply of double-deckers with manual gearboxes could no longer be maintained, the testing authorities agreed to conduct split tests, using a manual gearbox single-decker for one part, and a double-decker with semi-automatic transmission for the other part of the test. As a result, the use of Leyland Atlanteans for training became practical, and two of the four ex-British Airways vehicles were particularly associated with these duties. Number 954 (LYF 318D) is seen here in 1984 on Stranmillis Embankment, which then featured on the official test route.

R Bell

Engineering vehicles

Several Leyland Tiger PS1 half-cab single-deckers were retained for miscellaneous, non-service duties. Number 674 (GZ 6154), still in UTA colours, is seen performing as a towing vehicle in Lurgan in September 1974, recovering Leyland Atlantean 919 (COI 919), then the largest type of vehicle in the fleet. This Atlantean survives in preservation. *H Cunningham*

Another Leyland PS1, No 8517 (GZ 7585), was favoured with Ulsterbus colours for its towcar duties in Armagh depot, also photographed in September 1974. This vehicle has also been preserved. *H Cunningham*

Leyland PS1 571 (GZ 6124) was painted blue in October 1967 to act as a mobile training unit, before it also became a towcar at Lisburn.   *H Cunningham*

Several vehicles of the ex-Ribble Leyland Royal Tiger type later became depot towcars; No 9036 (ERN 723) was newly prepared for such work when photographed at Ballymena in 1971. Its smart appearance is enhanced by restoration of the aluminium side moulding which had been overpainted blue on the service livery. Such individual treatments were characteristic of the engineering vehicles. The adjacent Bedford, 126 (126 GZ) was the last of that type to operate in service, four years later.   *H Cunningham*

An unlikely candidate for retention and repainting from the Coastal Bus Service fleet, acquired in 1974, was their oldest vehicle, No 9041 (JWO 122). This was a 23-year-old Leyland Royal Tiger with unusual Lydney body, which had originated with Red and White of Chepstow. This received Ulsterbus colours as a towcar, based in Omagh, and survived for another four years.

I Houston

Left: Later in life, Leyland Tiger Cubs also joined the Engineering Department fleet as towcars. Number 372 (UZ 7372), based at Smithfield, was photographed at Great Victoria Street garage in 1979.

R Bell

Number 533 (OCS 733) was one of many of the ex-Western SMT Leyland Leopard L1s which enjoyed an extended life as a towcar, based in this case at Downpatrick. *I Houston*

Despite light weight, the short length and manual gearbox characteristics of the Bedford YRQs were well suited to towing duties, and several were retained in this capacity long after their service life ceased. Number 1748 (HOI 1748) was thus engaged when photographed in Great Victoria Street depot in 1985.

R Bell

The heavy recovery vehicle inherited from the UTA was this Leyland Hippo MkII (GZ 9030) which had been purchased in 1948, possibly from military sources. It remained in use until 1970 and is seen here recovering Leyland Leopard 1310 (4010 WZ), which was new in 1969, on the Upper Newtownards Road near Ballyhackamore. Foreman Shunter John Hinds (right) is checking the hitch before moving off.   *WH Montgomery*

For more complex recovery tasks, Ulsterbus maintained Ford recovery vehicles at the Duncrue Street workshops and later in Coleraine. The Irish Transport Trust Bus and Coach Rally became an annual opportunity for the Belfast-based vehicle to be displayed to the public and to provide back-up for any vehicle which developed a defect. Ford D800, BOI 7219, dating from 1970, is shown on display at the 1981 rally. The vehicle was transferred to Coleraine in 1983 and later re-registered LXI 7010 by the DVLA.   *R Bell*

The next Duncrue Street-based recovery vehicle, Ford Cargo CXI 6200, of 1983, arrives in Belfast from Coleraine with No 1578, which suffered severe accident damage in January 1987. *R Bell*

One of several miscellaneous vehicles retained by Ulsterbus engineering was this Atkinson articulated tanker. This was used to maintain supplies of diesel between depots and to set up emergency fuelling facilities after depot bomb attacks. The tractor unit was subsequently preserved. *R Bell*

Experiments and modifications

Leyland Leopard No 1520 (DOI 1520), delivered in May 1972, was the first bus to be fitted with forced air ventilation, deleting the need for opening ventilators on the windows. This was adopted as a standard production feature from 1975 on Leyland Leopards and Bristol RELLs. *R Bell*

Another experimental modification was this livery variant with less blue on the side panels. It was tried out in September 1972 on Leyland Leopard No 1578 (DOI 1578) and later adopted on production Bristol LHs and Bedford YRQs and YRTs. However, it was not deemed successful in the longer term, and the 224 buses concerned subsequently reverted to the established livery. *R Bell*

This remarkable looking vehicle was the result of a research programme using models in a wind tunnel to devise a front end shape to minimise air resistance in the interest of fuel economy. The resultant design was built onto the front end of No 179 (VOI 179) to allow full-scale validation of the research findings. Whilst the design was not practical for normal operation, there is significant similarity with the designs of vehicles such as the High Speed and Eurostar trains and the Wright Contour coach, which followed similar research. The vehicle did not operate in service in this form, but was displayed at the 1982 ITT Bus and Coach Rally at Bangor, where it was photographed. *P Savage*

Number 1140 (LXI 7140), delivered early in 1988, was experimentally fitted with an electronic destination display, showing service 130 to Ballymena in this shot outside Larne bus station. *P Savage*

The toll of destruction

No book on Ulsterbus covering the period of the Troubles in Northern Ireland would be complete without some reference to the destruction of buses in street riot situations and in malicious bomb and arson attacks on depots.

Two of the former UTA AEC Reliance buses specially built for the city services in Londonderry are seen at the parking ground on Foyle Road after an arson attack in September 1970.

R Bell

The shell of Leyland Leopard/Plaxton coach No 578 (COI 578), which had been reallocated to express services, was photographed after an attack on Pennyburn depot, Londonderry, in February 1978.

I Houston

The morning after an attack on buses parked in the yard at Donaghadee, County Down, in August 1980, when five buses were totally destroyed, including Leyland Leopards Nos 1365, 1414, 1411 and 1355. The tyres of 1411 are still smouldering.

R Bell

After the final destruction of Smithfield bus station and depot in September 1978, services were operated from temporary stands on Laganbank Road adjoining Oxford Street bus station. The fleet was augmented with vehicles borrowed from Citybus, including this former Potteries' Daimler Fleetline with Alexander 'W'-type body, No 2930 (BEH 154H) which is being directed by Inspector Jim Collins.

M Collins

The scene at Ballymoney, County Antrim, after the arson attack on 5 June 1981 in which nine buses were destroyed. The toll included one Leyland Atlantean, three Leyland Leopards, two Bristol RELLs and three Bedford YRQ and YLQs.

R Bell

Major private hire events

Ulsterbus is unusual among British bus undertakings in handling huge events, involving private hire of up to several hundred vehicles, on a very regular basis. The first such event to test the new Ulsterbus management occurred at Easter 1967 with the transport of the Junior Orange Institution from Belfast and surrounding areas to Larne. One side of the A8 dual carriageway, which was still under construction, was reserved for bus parking. The fleet employed on this occasion was almost exclusively of double-decked vehicles. Blue livery was still the exception rather than the rule. *Author*

The Orange Order's annual celebration on 12 July is a major event, with parades held simultaneously at many locations across the province. This photograph shows the bands and lodges assembling at Limavady for their transport to Coleraine in 1968. *Author*

The Apprentice Boys parade in Londonderry is also held annually, on or around 12 August, and assembles scores of buses from all parts of the province. I was responsible for the arrangements in 1968, when the track-bed of the former GNR(I) railway at Letterkenny Road was used to park all the visiting vehicles.   *Author*

Another view of the same occasion, taken from the east side of the Foyle, gives a panoramic impression of the scale of the operation. More than 150 buses can be identified.   *R Whitford*

The largest private hire operation in the history of Ulsterbus occurred in 1979 in connection with the Papal visit to Ireland. Over 700 buses from Ulsterbus and Citybus carried groups to the services held in Drogheda, Dublin, Limerick, Galway and Knock over two days. This view shows Ulsterbus vehicles at the Phoenix Park venue in Dublin.   *M Corcoran*

Advertising liveries

An early application of the overall advertising idea was applied to this Leyland Leopard rebuild No 1438 (COI 1438), decorated in 1976 to promote express coach services operated by the company. The messages included internal, cross-border and cross-channel destinations. The bus was destroyed again in the Smithfield depot fire in 1978. *Ulsterbus*

The sheer size of the Leyland Atlantean double-decker gave plenty of scope to the designer of this advertisement promoting the Sealink ferry route between Larne and Stranraer. Application of the design was entirely hand painted, carried out in Duncrue Street workshops by craftsman signpainter Terry Sharp (inset). *M McMaster/Ulsterbus*

Shopping centres were quick to take up the concept of the overall advertising bus to promote their trade around their local areas. Ballymena's Tower Centre was publicised by this design on Leyland Leopard No 107 in 1984.

Ulsterbus

Also in 1984, Bristol RELL No 2587 carried this colourful design promoting Craigavon Centre.

Ulsterbus

Timetable books

Initially, Ulsterbus continued the former UTA practice of publishing single provincewide timetable books. The first book, dated for 17 April 1967 (1), had a rather uninspiring blue cover with an artist's line drawing of one of the Leyland Leopard coaches recently acquired from Western Scottish and the Mourne Mountains. A second issue, in September 1967 (2), featured a new and brighter cover design featuring a line drawing of the first of the new Bedford/ Duple buses at Dunluce Castle. These books retained the original page size of 6.5" by 5", as used by the UTA, but the following year saw the adoption of the larger A5 size, 8.5" by 5.5", which had been adopted by all the major bus operators nationally, and included adoption of the 24-hour clock. A further improvement in the quality of the cover design followed the review of corporate design applications in 1969 (3).

At this time, timetables were being published once a year, generally in June, with intermediate changes being advertised locally on leaflets and notices. In 1972, however the publication was broken down into four regional books which were generally published twice yearly, on staggered dates. This permitted quicker publication of the books, reducing the risk of the timetable information being superseded before it was even printed, and spreading the administrative effort more evenly over the year. The cover design featured a map showing the extent of the region covered by each issue and the regions were colour coded: red, blue, green, and brown (4). In addition, each successive issue featured a change of shade of these colours, so that staff would instantly distinguish the new issue from the previous one when answering public enquiries.

A new cover design in 1976 featured the latest bus front-end design (5). In the same year, Newtownabbey became a fifth region for timetable purposes. Another cover design appeared in 1983, again featuring the map of regional areas covered by each volume (6). From time to time other, more localised, timetable booklets were tested, but these did not achieve general adoption.

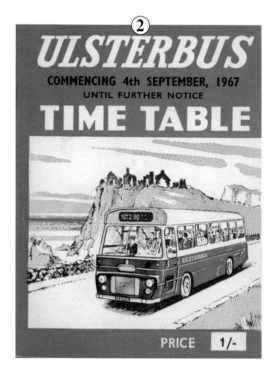

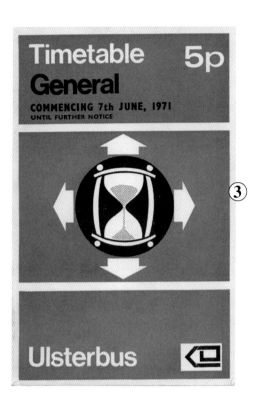

Timetable **5p**

General

COMMENCING 7th JUNE, 1971
UNTIL FURTHER NOTICE

Ulsterbus

③

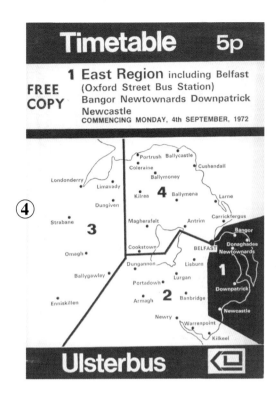

Timetable **5p**

1 **East Region** including Belfast
(Oxford Street Bus Station)
Bangor Newtownards Downpatrick
Newcastle
COMMENCING MONDAY, 4th SEPTEMBER, 1972

FREE
COPY

Ulsterbus

④

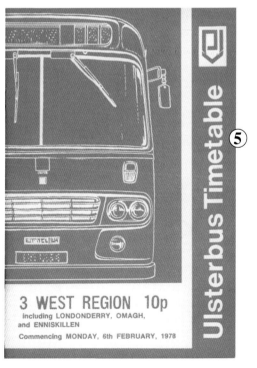

Ulsterbus Timetable

3 WEST REGION 10p
including LONDONDERRY, OMAGH,
and ENNISKILLEN

Commencing MONDAY, 6th FEBRUARY, 1978

⑤

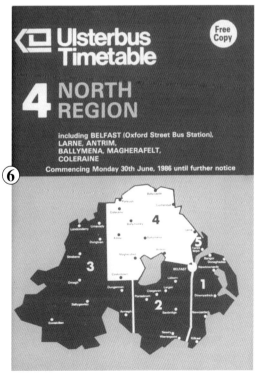

**Ulsterbus
Timetable**

Free
Copy

4 **NORTH
REGION**

including BELFAST (Oxford Street Bus Station),
LARNE, ANTRIM,
BALLYMENA, MAGHERAFELT,
COLERAINE
Commencing Monday 30th June, 1986 until further notice

⑥

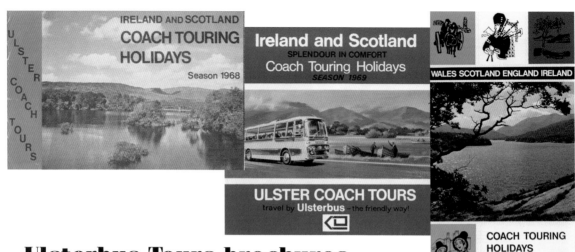

Ulsterbus Tours brochures

The annual Coach Holidays brochure was usually the most important marketing and publicity effort of the year. Although basic design themes were repeated for up to three years, new pictures and colours were introduced each year, to project from travel agency shelves an attractive and enticing image to potential clients. A large A4 page size was adopted as standard from 1972 onwards, while the expanding range of tours outgrew the traditional folders, to require staple bound multi-page books.   *Author's collection*

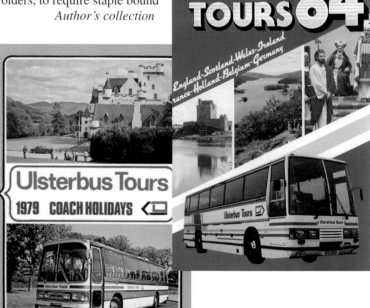

Open toppers

Former Citybus Daimler Fleetline No 2716 (716 UZ), which had been rebodied by Alexander (Belfast), was the vehicle chosen to become the first Ulsterbus open-top conversion in 1981, opening the seasonal service round the coastal route between Coleraine and the Giant's Causeway with support from Old Bushmills Distillery. In 1986 it was transferred to Bangor and opened a similar service between Bangor and Ballywalter. On this occasion it is acting as a mobile bandstand for Bangor's Friendship Band, entertaining visitors to the 1987 ITT Bus and Coach Rally.

JG Goan

The next open-top bus was based on former Citybus Leyland Atlantean No 2893 (JOI 2893), of 1976, which was converted in 1985 and took over the Causeway coast service the following year. This conversion retained shallow upper-deck windows in order to give passengers additional protection from the elements as it travelled along the frequently windy route along the cliff top between Portrush and Bushmills. It was photographed in Portrush.

R Bell

Bus stops

A feature of the early years of Ulsterbus was the wide variety of bus stop signs which existed around the province.

Signs inherited from the UTA included the reinforced concrete combined posts and signs. This design had originated around 1932 with the LMS/NCC bus services, and it is thought that the signs were manufactured 'in house' in a plant established to make concrete railway sleepers. Small numbers of these signs may have been erected by NIRTB, but they were again produced in large numbers around 1950 when the UTA implemented a major campaign to erect bus stops along most of the main arterial routes radiating from Belfast. These bear the words 'Bus Stop' or 'UTA Stage' (although 'Bus Stage' also exists). Many can still be seen on the Belfast–Kilkeel route and at a few other isolated locations. Other signs erected by the UTA were white enamelled iron plates bearing the single word 'Bus' in green, and mounted on tubular steel poles, often painted green and white. In rural areas and in the west of the province there were other means of indicating the location of bus stops. The word 'Bus' might be painted on a lamp-post, telegraph pole, or even a wooden post protruding from a hedge. There were also a number of towns, such as Bangor and Lurgan, where the former town councils had insisted upon their right to erect their own distinctive styles of bus stop signs.

Many unusual bus stops inherited by Ulsterbus survived for many years, including the concrete posts erected by the UTA (top left); those painted directly onto lamp-posts and telegraph poles (top right); and stops erected by local councils, such as Bangor (bottom left). Early Ulsterbus stops were often attached to convenient existing poles, as here in Carnlough (bottom right), or to trees near Dungannon (opposite page, top left). The version with the company name was mainly used in the Belfast area (opposite page, top right). *Author*

The standard sign adopted in 1979 was applied very widely. One of the most attractive bus stops in the province was in Ballinamallard, Co Fermanagh (bottom left), where the district council maintained a shelter and public toilets as well as seasonal floral baskets. The sign in Strabane (bottom right) is duplicated with a Bus Éireann stop, fabricated by adding their logo over an Ulsterbus stop plate.

Author

The first signs erected by Ulsterbus carried the word 'Bus' in large block letters in blue on an ivory background. These were manufactured from light sheet metal, which was rather susceptible to vandalism, and were later strengthened with metal bars top and bottom, or by mounting two plates bolted together for increased stiffness. In the Belfast area another form of the sign was introduced, adding the name 'Ulsterbus' above the word 'Bus', in order to avoid confusion with Belfast Corporation bus stops. Efforts were made to repaint the UTA stop poles from green to blue, and to freshen up some of the less conventional stops with new paint (usually yellow, for no identified reason).

In 1979 the company adopted the new bus stop design which was being proposed nationally, following the Warboys Committee review of road traffic signage. The now familiar sign incorporating a silhouette bus symbol also made provision for the operator's name, which was applied in white lettering on a blue bar using the corporate style of lettering current at that time. This design was used for all new and replacement signs which had to be erected in the years following and had become very widespread by 1988. However, there was no systematic programme to replace the older types of signage, except where damage or road realignment rendered it essential.

Ticket systems

Ulsterbus inherited the Setright ticket register system from the UTA. For almost all conductor operation, this was the 'Insert Setright' register, which endorsed the salient details of each issue on to a pre-printed card ticket inserted by the conductor into a slot on the front face of the register. The conductor carried a rack with different types of ticket blanks, distinguishable by colour as well as size and printed information. The range of the Insert register was 0–11s 11d, by penny steps. Halfpenny values were handled by use of tickets on which the halfpenny was pre-printed. An exception to the use of the Insert registers operated in Londonderry where conductors on the city services carried the 'Speed Model' Setright Register. This more modern and faster machine contained a partially printed roll of ticket paper within the register, on which the relevant details were printed by the register before the ticket was issued. The special registers in Londonderry were the 'low range' version, issuing fares up to 11½d, by halfpenny stages. Conductors in Larne also had the 'Speed' model Setright, because of the work performed on the Larne Town services.

For one-man operation, the UTA had purchased a quantity of the standard range 'Speed Model' Setrights, which could issue tickets over the range 0–19s 11½d by halfpenny steps. These also had the insert facility available, so that the register could validate pre-printed tickets of special types, such as weekly tickets. Sufficient registers had been ordered to handle the conversion of all single-deckers to one-man operation at the commencement of Ulsterbus, although there was little reserve.

The conversion to decimal currency, in February 1971, required considerable advance planning in order to have sufficient suitable registers available to handle decimal currency after 'D-day', without having to rely on making major alterations to several hundred registers on the day itself. Having a large surplus of Insert Setrights in store, and knowing that the requirement of machines suitable for conductor operation would have only a short future, the company carried out a simple refurbishment of Insert Setright registers, with a modification to limit the range to 0–99p. This enabled the entire stock of conductor registers to be exchanged overnight. On the tickets the former 'shillings and pence' spaces now read 'tens' and 'units' of new pence. The maximum fare imprinted in a single impression was effectively raised from 11s 11d in old currency (worth 59½p in the new) to 99p, a valuable benefit at a time of high inflation. It is probable that Ulsterbus was the only major undertaking to extend the life of its Insert Setright registers in this way, and a quantity of the modified registers was also supplied to the Lough Swilly company.

An 'Insert' Setright register converted for decimal currency in February 1971. These remained in use until 1972–3.   *Author*

The 'Speed', or 'Roll ticket' Setright register mounted on its motor unit was used by one-man operators for almost 20 years. (Conductors remaining between about 1973 and 1976 also used the 'Roll ticket' Setright manually.)   *Author*

The modifications required within the Speed Setright were much more complex. On these machines the old 'pence' dial was also replaced with units of new pence, while the old 'shillings' dial now read tens of new pence. The upper limit of 19s 11½d became 199 new pence, again a useful increase in the value of the largest ticket which could be issued in one operation. Indeed, Setright found that the 'mutilated gear' which was at the heart of the register, could take another position without major engineering work, thus allowing new registers to issue up to 209 pence, although this was not practical on modified registers. Ulsterbus were fortunate in that Setright had established a new factory in advance of decimalisation and had chosen Donegall Road, Belfast, as the location, so the source of parts and advice was readily accessible.

The opportunity had also been taken to purchase a large quantity of new Speed Setrights, equipped for decimal currency. Introducing these registers on 'D-day' allowed an equivalent number of omo (one-man operation) registers to be set aside for conversion over a longer time scale, so that they would eventually be brought back into use to replace the Insert registers as the conductor duties were converted to one-man operation. Further reserve capacity for the engineering work was obtained by the willingness of a number of omo drivers to use Insert registers for a few weeks over the change over period.

By the end of the decade, continuing inflation meant that despite the relief obtained by doubling the range of the Setright, the limit of £2.09 on a single issue was an embarrassment which could be overcome only by issuing multiple tickets to each passenger on long routes. The solution to that problem was to change over progressively to the Almex model A ticket register, a well-engineered machine capable of issuing fares up to £9.99 in a single operation. Another advantage over the Setright was that the Almex retained an audit roll containing the salient details of each ticket issued. This was very useful in researching discrepancies in drivers' cash, and would reveal and explain simple errors in a way which the Setright, which had simply cumulated a driver's takings, could not. There was also a limited number of a more sophisticated version of the Almex register, known as the PDR, which retained a second audit record on magnetic tape. This could be analysed by computer,

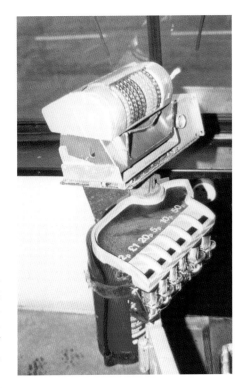

Top: The Almex PDR model of register was used by one driver in each depot to electronically gather more complex ticket sales statistics. The rather cumbersome stand was necessary to allow the register to be fitted above the standard Setright motor unit.
Author

Bottom: The more compact Almex Model A register was introduced in most depots from about 1980 onwards.   *Author*

allowing the company to obtain statistics of fares and patronage never before achievable. This group of registers had been introduced before decimalisation to carry out a special survey of patronage and was brought back into use in 1973 to maintain a sample survey of concessionary issues.

At a later stage, the use of Almex model 'A' registers in depot offices was also introduced, reducing sharply the range of specially printed tickets and, in the case of season tickets, handwritten blank tickets, held in stock at each location.

Even before the conversion to Almex was complete, the company was showing an interest in a new generation of electronic ticket registers. The model chosen was the Wayfarer MkII, which was introduced from 1986 onwards; it had replaced the remaining Setrights and was starting to replace the Almex registers as the period covered by this book was coming to an end. The first batch of Wayfarers were tested in Antrim depot, although these registers, which printed on thermal paper, were replaced by a version containing a ballistic printer before the general implementation programme commenced.

The Wayfarer MkII register, introduced progressively from 1986 onwards, marked the full transition into electronic technology. *Author*

Decimalisation

Both the United Kingdom and the Republic of Ireland changed over to decimal currency (pounds and new pence instead of pounds, shillings and pence) on 15 February 1971. Ulsterbus was certainly unusual, if not unique, in producing a staff training booklet which described and illustrated the currency issues of both countries, as Irish coinage circulated quite freely in Northern Ireland at the time. Indeed this continued for many years until Ireland entered the European Monetary System, when the British pound (Sterling) and the Irish pound (Punt) began to fluctuate in value. Since then, Ulsterbus drivers on cross-border services had to work with dual-currency fares lists and accept either currency from passengers. Tickets for cross-border journeys always show the Sterling value of the fare.

Tickets

Insert Setright Register

Pre decimalisation	Single (pink)	**1**
	Return (white)	**2**
	Weekly (red)	**3**
Post decimalisation	Single (pink)	**4**
	Weekly (green)	**5**

Roll Ticket Setright Register

Pre decimalisation   Single **6**
Return and weeklies
– as Insert Register

Post decimalisation   Single **7**
Weeklies – as Insert Register
Returns were issued from Roll

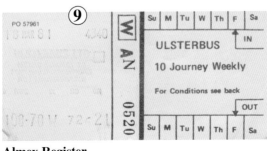

Almex Register

| Single | **8** | Weekly (yellow) **9** |

Wayfarer Register
Roll ticket issue
only **10**

Ulsterbus staff

Ulsterbus Tours frequently secured trophies at the annual Bus and Coach rallies. After the 1985 Rally, tour driver Pat McAllinney proudly displays the Concours d'Elegance trophy secured with No 543 (EXI 5543) which was first registered for that season. *Author*

After inspecting the new coach (1987 Leyland Tiger/ Duple 340, No 534, JXI 534), tour drivers Pat Melia (originally Citybus), John Finningham (Stranraer), John McLaughlin (Belfast) and John Duffy (Enniskillen) pose for the camera. Inside the coach are Barney Keenan and Maurice Donaldson (Bangor).

Author

Senior staff of the Tours Department (Glengall Street). Irvine Millar (Projects Manager) makes a presentation to Frances McComb (Administrator of Extended Tours) on the occasion of her retirement in 1981. Also in the group are Ken Thompson (Tours Manager), Stanley Bennett (Northern Ireland Tourist Board), Reg Ludgate (Publicity), Harry Gough (Travel Office Manager), and Hugh Dempster (Inspector, Tours and Private Hire).

Ulsterbus

Engineering staff at Enniskillen posing for the camera around 1985 comprise depot engineer Noel McLaughlin (left) with coachbuilders Daniel McAnespie and Kenny Nixon.

Author collection

Premises

During the early years of the company, Ulsterbus continued, in the main, to use bus stations and engineering garages which had been inherited from the UTA. Ownership of these premises had been transferred to the Northern Ireland Transport Holding Company, which charged an economic rental for each site. Naturally, Ulsterbus tried to reduce its use of former UTA sites to the minimum necessary to run an efficient and economic service, with the result that several traditional bus sites were officially vacated, including the former Belfast Omnibus Company's North Street yard, which had been used latterly as an overflow parking area for Smithfield. For this reason, Smithfield operations concentrated entirely on double-deckers, and its former single-decker operations were transferred to Great Victoria Street. Likewise, the former shared sites at Grosvenor Road and Duncrue Street (Road Running Shop) were vacated for the exclusive use of Northern Ireland Carriers. The Holding Company had the opportunity and responsibility to sell or let any premises not required for transport purposes by their subsidiaries. It was to be several months after the North Street yard was occupied by the Post Office before it was discovered that the Ulsterbus Conductors Training School, which had previously had to vacate Queen's Quay railway station, was still comfortably ensconced in the former UTA Passenger Manager's office!

As with vehicle replacement, improvements to these premises had to be financed from the turnover and surplus earned by the new company, but nevertheless early plans were made to start a refurbishment programme which soon developed to include new buildings and, in some cases, new sites.

One of the first places to be tackled was Londonderry, where the public bus station, as well as administrative offices and fuelling and cleaning functions, were squeezed into the former Victoria Market site at Strand Road, rented from the City Corporation. Space was so limited that overnight parking of buses spread across the adjacent quays. Relations with the Corporation were poor, following the company's unilateral termination of the agreement for operation of the city services, originally established by HMS Catherwood in 1929. This agreement had given the Corporation a share of 'profits', calculated by an outdated formula which continued to give a payment long after the services were proven to be losing money. The Corporation gave Ulsterbus notice to quit occupation of Victoria Market early in 1968, and the company had to identify alternative premises within a very short timescale. Fortunately, the Corporation accepted that the city should still have a public bus station convenient to the commercial centre, and agreed to a division of another former market, the Butter Market site on Foyle Street, between a public bus station and a car park. Ulsterbus set up this bus station with a temporary building, intended to last 5–6 years, but which actually survived for 20 years before being replaced by a modern building on the same site. Other temporary sites were found along Foyle Street to accommodate the Area Office, the bus wash and a parking area created on former railway land along Foyle Road, where the Foyle Valley Railway Museum is now situated. Only the bus maintenance garage was unaffected. This was sited on Foyle Street adjacent to the former GNR(I) railway station, which had closed in 1965, and was therefore already convenient to the grouping of functions in Foyle Street.

Soon after this, work started on a number of projects to upgrade premises or provide replacement buildings at most bus depots. A standard design evolved which provided the necessary facilities quite economically in a simple flat-roofed grey-brick depot building, which can best be described as functional rather than attractive. Just as with fleet replacement, the philosophy was straightforward – the limited funds available had to be spread as widely as possible to improve facilities for staff and passengers alike.

At Larne, the new facilities were built on a new site, replacing the remarkably central site of the former narrow gauge railway, which had been closed in 1950. Larne was one of the few main stations on the former LMS–NCC rail system which had not had an integrated bus and railway station operation, so it was a step forward when Ulsterbus obtained this former railway goods yard site on Circular Road adjoining the railway station. This co-ordination was short-lived, however, as Northern Ireland Railways relocated their station and

The first of a series of new bus stations to a standard design was that in Circular Road, Larne, completed in 1970. This photograph shows it many years later, after removal of the original railway station and construction of the elevated harbour highway, visible in the background. *Author*

This new bus station building in Bangor, completed in 1971, replaced an earlier building on the same site. *R Whitford*

These premises at Enniskillen, completed in 1971, replaced an old building on Belmore Street, and provided both a new bus station building and a new garage, visible in the background. This photograph was taken almost twenty years after the new station opened. *Author*

even the railway alignment a few years later, to facilitate construction of the elevated Harbour Highway. The new Ulsterbus depot building provided a public bus station, with all staff facilities, and also a new engineering garage and vehicle wash bay, together with generous parking on a single site, opening in November 1970. On the same date a simpler building opened at Ballyclare, which is operated as a sub-depot under the control of Larne. Public facilities were minimal here, but staff had a mess room and toilet, and a vehicle wash shelter was provided. This was also located on part of a former railway site, but the original station buildings were released for alternative uses.

The next new depot to be opened was at Edward Street, Newry, in June 1971, again a former railway site. Facilities here comprised a new engineering garage, parking area, and a depot building providing staff facilities. This site did not offer public bus station facilities, as service departures continued to operate from the Mall, closer to the town's shopping centre, although these stops provided only minimal shelter for passengers' comfort.

In October of the same year, a new bus station building opened on the existing site at Bangor, which adjoined the railway station, although the old stone-built engineering garage, which could barely accommodate 11 m buses, was to remain in use for many years.

Another complete depot was constructed in Enniskillen, also in 1971. Here, the garage building was piled on low land close to Lough Erne, while the standard low bus station building was later made even less significant by construction of the new highway by-passing the town centre. Downpatrick depot opened next, in January 1972, on a site close to the commercial centre of the town at Market Street. Once again, the small bus station building was barely adequate for the numbers of passengers crowding in each afternoon, while the garage opposite (as in Enniskillen) was designed to take only single-decker buses. Already, double-deckers were considered to have no future role in rural areas.

In 1975 a major work in Londonderry came to fruition with the opening at Pennyburn of the large engineering garage, fuelling and washing facility, and bus parking area, together with a two-storey office building. The site proved very expensive to develop, due to the depth of peat below its 'greenfield' surface. This development allowed the various temporary servicing facilities, established in 1968–9 along Foyle Street, to be vacated, leaving only the bus station as the focus of public interface with the company.

A very similar site and layout was developed for the new depot at Craigavon – Highfield. In line with the

This new maintenance garage at Newry, completed in 1971, was typical of the standard design applied in several locations. However, at some rural depots which no longer operated double-deckers, the opportunity was taken to lower the entrance doors and overall height to suit only single-deckers. *Author*

Work in progress during 1977 on the site of Craigavon depot in the Highfield commercial area of the designated 'new town'. This was completed in 1978. Marlborough House government offices can be seen in the background, through the 'skeleton' of the two-storey building which was to house the depot and area offices.

Ulsterbus

Conversion of a former railway house provided this attractive bus station in Newcastle, opened in 1979.

Ulsterbus

Craigavon 'new town' concept, Highfield was designed to replace garages and operational facilities at both Portadown and Lurgan. The large garage and parking area, on a greenfield site on the edge of the 'new town's' designated 'commercial' zone, also featured a two-storey office block accommodating the Area office, but was not envisaged as a public access site. It opened in summer 1978.

Ballymena also received a new bus station building with a two-storey block to accommodate the Area office. Although the bus area adjoined the railway station, the opportunity was taken to separate the bus station activity to the opposite side of the yard, and those of the bus staff who had occupied rooms in the rail station buildings now moved across. The development included a new engineering garage at the far end of the site, removed from passenger activity.

Around this time, in recognition of the investment which Ulsterbus had made in upgrading premises, the Northern Ireland Transport Holding Company discontinued the rental system, although ownership of the properties, including the new buildings, continued to rest with them.

Another new bus station development on an existing site adjoining a railway station was completed early in 1979, at Coleraine. Here, the new engineering garage was on the opposite side of the tracks, where a steam locomotive shed had previously stood. Improvements were also carried out at Antrim, which was upgraded to full depot status, after having been operated as a sub-depot of Ballymena since the formation of Ulsterbus. Here the bus station adjoins the rail station, and Ulsterbus offices are accommodated within the station building.

This aerial photograph of the Oxford Street bus station, taken around 1987, shows the bus station site, the bus parking and refuelling area and the vacant land then available from the former Mays Market area. The relationship of the bus station site to the alignment of Chichester Street (top centre of picture) indicates its proximity to the city centre. This entire site was subsequently redeveloped as part of the Laganside project, incorporating the Waterfront Hall.

Ulsterbus

Around the same time, the bus station at Newcastle was moved out of the small corner it still occupied of the town's rather grandiose railway station building, which was needed for a supermarket development. A compact bus station was devised in the ground floor of the former stationmaster's house just along the street, doubly convenient as the engineering garage already existed on the same piece of land.

Meanwhile in Belfast, there had been a succession of proposals to combine the three bus station sites, at Great Victoria Street, Oxford Street and Smithfield, onto one site, but with little sign of agreement among the various planning authorities involved. The 1969 Belfast Transportation Plan recommended a single bus station on the Smithfield site, enlarged by the addition of the Smithfield Square market area. However, this site was not large enough and attention switched to the Great Victoria Street site when the railway moved out to the Central Station development after 1976. This site is traversed by the Boyne Bridge, where the road authorities planned to build a new road system at ground level which would have left the bisected site unworkable as a combined bus station and depot. By 1978, consideration was being given to the Oxford Street site, which could have been enlarged by incorporating the derelict Mays Market area. Proximity to Central Station was seen as a potential advantage. However, City councillors had envisioned a large concert hall on the Oxford Street site, visible from the front of City Hall, a plan which effectively blighted the Oxford Street site.

All this indecision resulted in considerable reluctance to spend substantial sums of money on short-term improvements, although some reconstruction was carried out at Smithfield in November 1970. Both Smithfield and Great Victoria Street suffered bomb damage early in 1972, and all three depots were hit by car bombs on 'Bloody Friday', 21 July 1972, with serious loss of life at Oxford Street. Repairs were carried out as quickly as possible. Smithfield was hit again in September 1978; this time the whole depot was destroyed by fire and was not rebuilt. Staff and vehicles were transferred to Oxford Street depot, although additional stands were needed for service departures on the adjoining Laganbank Road. The strategic value of retaining two bus stations in Belfast was now recognised within the company. It was not until late in the 1980s that the way forward became

Coleraine bus station was built in 1979. The office replaced an older building on the same site.

Ulsterbus

The passenger waiting area at Coleraine, although generous in size, afforded little comfort or shelter by more modern standards.

Ulsterbus

clearer, and plans began to be made for redevelopment of Great Victoria Street on the existing site, but without the objective of consolidating the Oxford Street activity into the same site. By this time the situation at Great Victoria Street was complicated by the desire of the railway company, also owned by the NITHC, to undo the mistakes of the 1970s by reopening a railway station on this site, with a spur track off their main line. This was clearly going to reduce the space available to Ulsterbus but at least the Road Service had pulled back from their determination to divide the site at the Boyne Bridge.

The final new depot to be constructed during the era covered by this volume was at Beechvalley, Dungannon (a former railway station site), where a new public bus station replaced the old stands and tiny office in the Square. A new garage also replaced the inherited site on Ballygawley Road. In the case of the bus station building, although the layout was similar to those which had already been built, the appearance was radically changed for the better by the adoption of a pitched roof and the use of red rustic brick rather than the light grey which had been so widely used before. These facilities were officially opened on 10 December 1984.

Ulsterbus livery

During 1966, the management team for the new Ulsterbus undertaking gave thought to the bus livery for the new undertaking. To emphasise the break from the past, it was keen to move away from the green which had been associated with both the NIRTB and the UTA, while red buses would be confused with those of Belfast Corporation. Blue seemed to be a suitable alternative. After experimenting with Oxford blue, which had in the past been used by the Great Northern Railway (Ireland) and still featured on Dublin City buses, it was decided to adopt a lighter shade, known as Riviera blue, for the lower panels, with the contrast of Trader ivory for the roofs and window surrounds. The first vehicle to be painted in this scheme was ex-Edinburgh Tiger Cub No 9343, which also had the Ulsterbus fleet name applied in two different lettering styles, of which the upper case italic Roman squared serif style was preferred over a florid script. Most vehicles emerging from overhaul in the Central Workshops at Duncrue Street from late 1966 onwards bore these colours, although none entered service until January 1967.

To some extent, priority was given to repainting the younger vehicles in the inherited fleet, together with the recently acquired vehicles which had yet to be painted. It was expected that repainting of the entire fleet would take between two and three years to complete and that some of the older types would have been replaced by new vehicles within that timescale, so that labour devoted to repainting these would be wasted. Thus only one of the low-bridge double-deckers was repainted. Even that (No 944) was a local effort at Coleraine depot on the insistence of a PSV inspector. Only limited numbers of the Royal Tiger single-deckers were repainted, mainly because they underwent a heavy overhaul which included removal of their heavy wooden roof-racks and rear ladders. Indeed, the last vehicle to wear the UTA livery was Royal Tiger No 8984, which was withdrawn late in 1971, so a few examples of that livery survived longer than originally anticipated, due mainly to the effect of vehicle losses on the renewal programme.

Initially, the Ulsterbus name was applied to the middle of the side panels in large (10") lettering. However, when it was found that this size could not be accommodated on the new Bedford/ Duple coaches, a smaller (5" high) version was adopted and applied higher on the waistband of these vehicles. This size and mounting position was then adopted for general application.

One of the new 1967 Bedford/Duple coaches (No 9264) was sent back to Duple for a replacement body following an accident early in 1968 and was returned with an experimental variant of the colour scheme – an additional broad band of ivory along the body side, following the manufacturer's mouldings. This proved sufficiently popular to be adopted as the standard for new vehicles from 1968 onwards. Indeed, the pattern of the side panel joints and mouldings on the new Potter bodies was designed to suit the application of this livery. The change was applied retrospectively to the entire fleet of Bedford/Duples as they came up for overhaul. The decision also resulted in some changes in application of the new colours to former UTA vehicles, with greater sympathy for the original body mouldings.

Initially, it had been intended to retain the UTA special coaching livery of two shades of blue (dark Oxford and pale Elizabethan) exclusively for the luxury touring coaches, together with the new brand name 'Ulster Coach Tours'. The new Plaxton coaches purchased for the launch of the new undertaking were specified and delivered accordingly. However, this decision was reversed in 1968, when the existing UTA coaches were repainted in standard ivory and riviera blue, although it was to be three years before the new vehicles were brought into line. The Ulster Coach Tours name was also discontinued after the 1968 season and replaced by Ulsterbus Tours, as it was apparent that the new company name had achieved widespread recognition while the Ulster Coach Tours name was not recognised as belonging to the same stable.

By 1969 the board had decided that the corporate presentation of the company needed improvement and greater consistency. Consultants recommended a range of improved styles, many of which were adopted as far as stationery and brochures were concerned. The corporate logo was introduced at this time and was added to the vehicle livery as a symbol applied alongside the fleet name on the waistband. However, the revised style of lettering in upper and lower case Folio type was not adopted for the general fleet, and for many years appeared only on luxury coaches.

The next change in livery was in 1972, when fleet No 1578 was turned out in a predominantly ivory livery, with two narrow blue bands. This was adopted as the livery for the 223 lightweight rural buses delivered over the next two years, but it soon proved less than practical, showing up road dirt badly, and was discontinued in 1975. All buses bearing this predominantly ivory livery were returned to standard over the following year or two.

A major relaunch of marketing of express services was undertaken in 1976, with a distinctive black 'Ulsterbus Express' logo designed 'in house' by myself, which could be used on timetables, leaflets, posters and featured on the express coaches themselves. Initially this was intended to be used only on vehicles designed specifically for express services, but in practice it was used more widely, on most of the 'semi-luxury' Leopards delivered from 1976 on, as these often operated services in the express category. It also gave a superior image to vehicles which were used on private hire and local tours.

In 1977 the opportunity was taken to change the base colour of luxury coaches from ivory to white, and the blue to a slightly darker and richer shade. The coach livery was revised again in 1983, with the arrival of the Duple Caribbeans which had a new style of livery with an upswept stripe toward the rear, and reintroduced an additional and lighter shade of blue. Both blue shades were standard colours in the Ford Transit range of vans at that time.

Although the 'Folio' lettering style had been adopted for publicity and coaches, no further attempt was made to introduce it on service buses until the launch of the first Leyland Tiger, with Alexander 'N'-type body in 1984. This was not considered successful, however, and a more forceful typeface (upper case 'Microgramma') was adopted instead, although this was not used on any other vehicle types. These vehicles also introduced significant changes in the livery style, with more blue on the upper area of the body, including the front dome, the cove panels and the window pillars, although the horizontal surface of the roof itself remained ivory. The ivory band along the bodyside was deeper, starting from the waist rail, thus deleting the blue waistband. The fleet name and logo had been switched to the cove panel above the windows to maintain the contrast.

Duple Caribbean 550 (EXI 5550) of 1984 shows the strikingly distinctive livery created for this type of coach, including the stylised 'U' shape on the rear panel. The glazed name panel on the rear was one of few visible differences between the 1983 and 1984 purchases of caribbean bodywork. *Thomson*

The basic service bus seat, with double stainless-steel top rail, was finished in plain black leathercloth, as shown on Leyland Leopard No 1520. The same effect was applied to the lightweight Bristols and Bedfords and the Bristol RELLs. *Author*

The original choice of red/grey/black moquette and its application to semi-luxury seats is shown in this view of one of the first group of Leyland Leopards, delivered in 1969. *H Cunningham*

Interior trim

The interior ambience of a bus is very much determined by the choice of seating fabric and of sympathetic colours for paintwork and ceiling and panelling surfaces. For many years, the predecessor undertakings had chosen green fabrics and paint colours in sympathy with their green exterior liveries, although in the latter few years blue fabric was used in blue-liveried vehicles. The new Ulsterbus management team took a different viewpoint – that the exterior and interior colours were not seen together and that prime consideration should be given to selecting interior colour schemes which would be fresh and different, as well as comfortable and welcoming, without necessarily being of similar colours to the exterior. The first choice was of a red, grey and black moquette fabric for seats on semi-luxury, express and touring-quality coaches, with red seat frames and pale grey surfaces. This moquette choice continued to be used on new vehicles until about 1977, and indeed reappeared (to use up stocks of fabric held in store) on new Flexibus coaches between 1984 and 1988. Basic service buses had red and black panelled seats in 'Ambla', a soft leathercloth material.

Many of the subsequent changes to interior materials were in response to the constant problem of vandalism. The company tried to reduce the cost of repairs to seating by simplifying the style of trim and reducing the variation in fabrics. For example, on basic service buses, the seats became plain black from 1970 on. Efforts were also made to make seats more resistant to damage. The shaped fibreglass seat panels were in this category, used for seat backrests in Ulsterbus basic buses from the mid-1970s and also for seat cushions on a few rear seats, although Citybus adopted the design more extensively. Ulsterbus managers were conscious not only that their passengers tended to make longer journeys, but also that it was generally difficult to confine vehicles to the school journeys on which the vandalism was more pronounced.

For similar reasons, the use of the traditional wool moquette fabric was discontinued in 1977 and replaced by a synthetic 'condura' fabric in black corduroy style. This was produced for the car industry at a much more economic price. However, as car manufacturers were changing their colours and styles annually, Ulsterbus could not secure long-term supplies of this material, and were obliged to accept in successive years, a different texture, then a brown colour from 1978. The final version, a mottled brown known as 'bitter chocolate', was maintained for several years from 1986 before it too became unavailable.

Meanwhile, a new yellow and brown moquette pattern was adopted for new luxury coaches purchased from Duple in 1974–6 and was also specified on express coaches from Duple and Plaxton from 1978 to 1981. The latest fashion for luxury coaches was a style with vertical stripes down each seat and this was adopted, in brown and yellow 'autumnal shades', for the Duple Dominant II and Plaxton Supreme coaches purchased from 1979 to 1981. Another new style, with grey base and vertical stripes of various colours including blue and yellow, was selected for the Caribbean coaches in 1983–4, although a brown and orange stripe fabric was specified for the Duple Laser and Wright Contour coaches. The pale grey-based fabric in the Caribbeans did not prove satisfactory in the longer term and towards the end of the period covered by this book, a different grey style incorporating a vertical stripe of yellow/ orange chevrons was adopted for luxury coaches, including later production of Flexibus conversions. The base colour for this fabric, in a pinstripe style of two shades of grey, was designed by myself and is believed to have been manufactured uniquely for Ulsterbus.

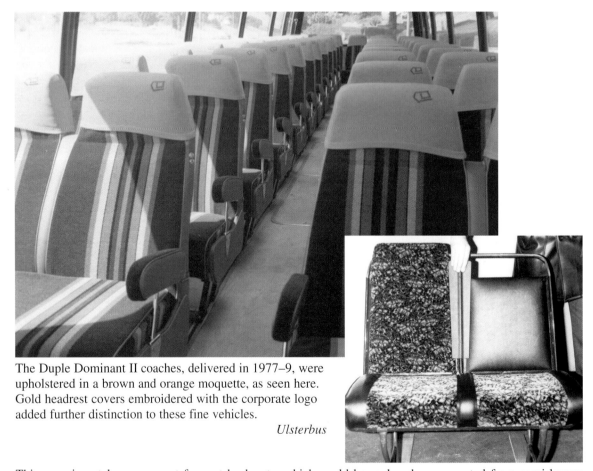

The Duple Dominant II coaches, delivered in 1977–9, were upholstered in a brown and orange moquette, as seen here. Gold headrest covers embroidered with the corporate logo added further distinction to these fine vehicles.

Ulsterbus

This experimental arrangement for seat backrests, which could be replaced or converted from semi-luxury standard to basic bus standard seat design in minutes, was designed by myself and fabricated in Duncrue Street workshops to test its feasibility.

Author

A restoration project

The company decided to mark the achievement of 50 years of public ownership of the province's bus services in 1985 in two ways. One was the publication of a book, assembled and edited by myself.

The other was by reconstructing an original NIRTB bus, as the number of vehicles surviving in preservation from that period was very small. A local enthusiast, Graham Reid, had rescued GZ 783, a Bedford OWB Utility bus of 1942 which had originally belonged to the NIRTB. After World War Two, the Board sold these buses off, finding a ready market on the mainland, particularly in Scotland and Wales. This vehicle was handled by dealers SMT Sales & Service, an offshoot of the SMT bus company.

The early postwar SMT coach body is hoisted on the powerful overhead cranes in Duncrue Street Workshops.

G laverty

The original body was scrapped and replaced with a new coach body, very similar in appearance to the contemporary Duple Vista, but built under licence by SMT in their own workshops. After working for several local operators in Scotland, it passed into the hands of a fruit farmer in Angus, who used several old buses and coaches to transport his seasonal staff. When this life was over, Graham purchased the vehicle and brought it back to Northern Ireland, but was unable to undertake much restoration.

At this point Ulsterbus

Meanwhile the original Bedford OWB chassis, dating from 1942, is removed for overhaul.

G Laverty

The timber body frame is assembled on the refurbished chassis.

G Laverty

stepped in, purchased the vehicle and set about a major restoration. As the post-war body was badly deteriorated, and anyway not original, it was lifted off the chassis and scrapped. The chassis was thoroughly cleaned and restored and a new body was constructed, replicating as closely as possible the original wartime Utility body design. Two foremen from Duncrue Street, Geordie Lavery and Alfie Clements, travelled with myself to visit and scrutinise several surviving Bedford OWBs in England. It transpired that none of these were fully restored, but they enabled the experts to photograph and measure up details of the construction. Critical help was provided by Cliff Burgess of the Portsmouth CTP 200 restoration project. He had established that his vehicle would also require a completely new body, as the original had deteriorated beyond repair. After our visit he completed the dismantling of the main body sections and brought the parts over to Belfast, where they were studied in detail and used as a template for the manufacture of replica body framing. A spare set of all parts was cut and shipped back to Portsmouth for the CTP 200 project.

Coachbuilder Jimmy Gordon is seen assembling parts of the timber framing for the body.

G Laverty

Another aspect of the project was the collection of dozens of photographs of Bedford OWBs in service as the work progressed, which became very useful in answering queries about details of the finish. Since the vehicle was restored, it has been maintained in roadworthy condition and appears

The body exterior panelling is almost complete. Drawings and dimensions for the original wartime utility bodywork were followed as faithfully as possible. *G Laverty*

periodically at rallies and parades, as well as having been on display in the Ulster Folk and Transport Museum.

The Portsmouth vehicle was completed by 1994, in good time to celebrate the fiftieth anniversary of the D-Day landings. A second former NIRTB Bedford, GZ 2248, has since been restored in England and operates in regular service for Green Bus Service of Rugely during the summer season.

Sheet metal worker John McCaughey manufactures seat frames, faithfully copied from an original which had survived as a garden seat at the Carnlough home of Inspector Sam Shannon.

G Laverty

Coachbuilder Billy Ferguson and sheet metal worker Geordie McCoy complete panelling of the roof.

G Laverty

Pictured at the conclusion of the project are Geordie Laverty (Foreman, body shop), Jimmy McMeekin (Senior Foreman), Michael McMaster (Foreman, paint shop), Jimmy Elliott (Works Manager) and Alfie McClements (Foreman, sheet metal shop).

Dromore Leader

Ulsterbus Managers 1966–88

This group photograph taken at the official opening of Dungannon's new bus station at Beechvalley, in December 1984, includes the Board and management staff (full list appended opposite top). *Ulsterbus*

1   Darwin Templeton, Director
2   Jimmy Macklin, Claims Officer, HQ.
3   Jimmy Elliott, Works Manager, Duncrue Street.
4   Billy Woods, Garage Engineering Manager.
5   Ronnie Moore, Director, McLaughlin & Harvey (Contractors).
6   Ronnie Houston, Managing Director, McLaughlin & Harvey.
7   Fay Dunlop, Director.
8   Sydney Catherwood, Chairman.
9   Peter Brand, Director.
10 Ellen Kelso, Revenue Accountant, HQ.
11 Joe O'Reilly, Depot Manager, Antrim.
12 John Kidd, DM, Dungannon.
13 Billy Brown, DM, Newtownards.
14 David Leathem, Trainee Manager.
15 Sam Thompson, Staff Officer.
16 Billy Dowds, Area Manager, Southern Area.
17 Tom Campbell, Chief Engineer, Citybus.
18 Bobby Wilson, Area Manager, Northern Area.
19 Brian Carson, Area Manager, Western Area.
20 Billy Hamilton, DM, Falls (Citybus).
21 Tom Andrews, Area Manager, Belfast Area.
22 Derrick Wilson, Accounts Dept, HQ.
23 Ted Hesketh, Company Secretary & Accountant.
24 Ken Middleton, Chief Engineer, Ulsterbus.
25 Werner Heubeck, Managing Director.
26 Tony Wylie, DM, Ballymena.
27 Dick Lockhart, Wages Office Manager, HQ.
28 Fred Buick, DM, Londonderry.
29 Jimmy Rocks, DM, Great Victoria Street.
30 Micky McLaughlin, Area Engineer, Western Area.
31 Brian McClean, DM, Omagh.
32 David Butler, Stores Manager, Duncrue Street.
33 Ian Cunningham, DM, Downpatrick.
34 Pat Deehan, Chief Driving Instructor, HQ.
35 Bobby Campbell, DM, Craigavon.
36 Jimmy Magill, DM, Newcastle.
37 John Preston, Contracts Manager, McLaughlin & Harvey.
38 Tom McClintock, Property Manager, HQ.
39 John McCready, Accountant, HQ.
40 Eric Fiddament, Technical Engineering Manager.
41 Tommy Brown, Engineer, Citybus.
42 John Kerrin, DM, Newry.
43 Eddie Rothwell, DM, Ardoyne (Citybus).
44 Sam Dowling, DM, Lisburn.
45 Eric Harvey, Purchasing Manager, HQ.
46 Billy Campbell, Chauffeur to M.D.
47 Billy Telford, DM, Bangor.
48 Irvine Millar, Projects Manager, HQ.
49 Conor O'Cleary, DM, Larne.
50 Alan Warburton, Computer Manager, HQ.
51 Bertie Steele, DM, Oxford Street.
52 David Tweed, DM, Coleraine.
53 Frank Clegg, DM, Short Strand (Citybus).
54 Ricky McArthur, DM, Enniskillen.
55 Andy Watt, DM, Magherafelt.
56 Joe Campbell, DM, Armagh.

Key to Staff photograph

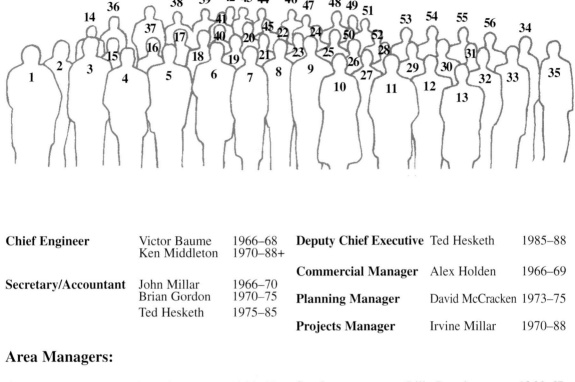

Chief Engineer	Victor Baume	1966–68
	Ken Middleton	1970–88+
Secretary/Accountant	John Millar	1966–70
	Brian Gordon	1970–75
	Ted Hesketh	1975–85

Deputy Chief Executive	Ted Hesketh	1985–88
Commercial Manager	Alex Holden	1966–69
Planning Manager	David McCracken	1973–75
Projects Manager	Irvine Millar	1970–88

Area Managers:

Central area	Hugh Waring	1966–67
	Billy Dowds	1967–78
Belfast area	Max Hale	1978–83
	Tom Andrews	1983–88+
Northern area	Bertie Roy	1966–80
	Bobby Wilson	1980–85
	Bertie Steele	1985–87
	Sam Dowling	1987–88+

Southern area	Billy Dowds	1966–67
	David McCracken	1967–73
	Bobby Wilson	1973–78
	Billy Dowds	1978–85
	Bobby Wilson	1985–88+
Western area	James Houston	1966–70
	Bill Ferris	1970–83
	Brian Carson	1983–88

Head Office:

Accountant	John McCreary	1985–86
	Brian Lyle	1986–88+
Staff Officer	Sam Thompson	1966–88+
Chief Driving Instructor		
	Paddy Deehan	1968–88+

Engineering:

Works Manager	Jimmy Elliott	1966–88
	Mal McGreevy	1988+
Garage Engineering Manager		
	Billy Woods	1970–87
Technical Engineering Manager		
	Eric Fiddament	1969–88+

Depot Managers:

Antrim	RJ McBride	1977–80		**Larne**	Jack Selwood	1970–72
	JO'Rielly	1980–88			James Houston	1972–75
	Dennis Kennedy	1988+			Billy Telford	1975–82
Armagh	Tommy Young	1966–84		**Lisburn**	Sam Dunlop	1966–67
	John J Campbell	1984–88+			Sam Dowling	1967–87
					Bobby Campbell	1987–88+
Ballymena	Frank Taggart	1966–72				
	Sandy Boyce	1972–80		**Londonderry**	Freddie Buick	1966–88
	RJ McBride	1980–84			David Leathem	1988+
	Tony Wylie	1984–88+				
				Lurgan	Austin Murphy	1966–68
Bangor	Harry Willis	1967–82				
	Billy Telford	1982–88+		**Magherafelt**	Bertie Steele	1966–67
					Hugh Kerr	1967–83
Coleraine	Johnnie McMaster	1966–72			Andy Watt	1983–88
	David Tweed	1972–86				
	Ricky McArthur	1986–88+		**Newcastle**	Jimmy Magill	1966–88
					Eileen Starkey	1988+
Craigavon	Bobby Campbell	1977–87				
	Randall Roderick	1987–88+		**Newry**	Bill Ferris	1966–70
					Jim Gray	1970–81
Downpatrick	George Thompson	1966–77			John Kerrin	1982–88
	Ian Cunningham	1977–87			PJ Darby	1988+
	Eileen Starkey	1987–88				
	Hugh Scott	1988+		**Newtownards**	Hugh Mitchell	1966–82
					Billy Brown	1982–88+
Dungannon	Gerry Mayne	1966–79				
	Billy Brown	1979–82		**Omagh**	Alec Young	1967–69
	John Kidd	1982–88+			Colin Townsley	1969–82
					Brian McClean	1982–88+
Enniskillen	George Breen	1966–79				
	Andy Watt	1979–83		**Oxford Street**	Jack Cambell	1966–79
	Ricky McArthur	1983–86			Bertie Steele	1979–85
	David Leathem	1986–88			Frank Clegg	1985–88
	Raymond Gault	1988+			Paddy Moss	1988+
Great Victoria Street	Tommy Hannon	1966–67		**Portadown**	Bobby Wilson	1967–73
	Bertie Steele	1967–75			Bobby Campbell	1974–77
	Jimmy Rocks	1975–87				
	Maurice Kennedy	1987–88+		**Smithfield**	Eddie Gaw	1966–67
					Jimmy Rocks	1967–75
Larne	Sam Niblock	1966–69			Bertie Steele	1975–79

+ indicates that these managers' tenure of office continued beyond the period covered by this volume.

Fleet list

The fleet list is divided into four sections. The first table lists in numerical order the official operational fleet inherited from the Ulster Transport Authority on 17 April1967. Buses built new for Ulsterbus Ltd from 1967 to 1988 are in the second table, broadly in chronological order. The third table covers minibuses built new for the Flexibus subsidiary. The fourth table comprises pre-owned vehicles purchased by Ulsterbus, in the majority of cases to replace vehicles lost due to civil disturbance. Since there are over 3000 vehicles are in these lists, the general descriptive data for each group of vehicles is presented in summary form, including a general indication of the longevity of each type in normal passenger service. Each section is followed by individual listing of those vehicles withdrawn from normal service during the period covered by this book. Vehicles continuing in service beyond 1988 will be listed in Volume 6 in this series. Withdrawal dates quoted refer to final withdrawal from normal passenger service. Many withdrawn vehicles remained in company ownership for lengthy periods, either held in reserve or as a source of spare parts. Code letters attached to the withdrawal year are explained at the start of the first such list. Appendices following the fleet list show vehicles retained for other active uses, ie towing, training and staff transport, with relevant dates. Another appendix lists the surplus vehicles inherited from the UTA for disposal. Although a few of these may have been operated by the new company, they were not included in the official fleet and were withdrawn by the end of June 1967.

PSV Circle codes to describe bodywork and seating are used in the column headed 'Seats' and are explained as follows:

B	Bus seating	F	Front or forward entrance
C	Coach seating	R	Rear entrance
DP	Dual-purpose (coach seating in bus body)	RD	Rear entrance with door
H	High-bridge double decker	D	Dual doorway (front entrance/centre exit)
L	Low-bridge double decker	T	Toilet
OT	Open-top double decker		

(Seating of double deckers is quoted as upper deck followed by lower deck.)

Where the symbol 'xxx' appears in the Reg No column, this indicates that the numbers on the plates do not run in sequence. The word 'various' indicates that the registration letters also vary. In both instances full details for individual vehicles will be found in the withdrawal lists. The symbol * indicates vehicles withdrawn before their normal lifespan.

Suffixes used in the withdrawal lists:

a	withdrawn due to accident	r	retained as garage towing vehicle
c	transferred to Citybus, Belfast	s	sold to another operator
f	withdrawn with accidental fire damage	t	retained as driver training vehicle
m	withdrawn due to malicious damage/destruction	n/o	not operated
p	preserved	u	retained for staff transport

(1) Ulsterbus vehicles inherited from the UTA on 17 April 1967

Fleet No	Reg No	Built	Chassis type	Body type	Seats	Wdn
1–3	8813–15 AZ	1961	Austin T200	UTA	B20F	1968–69
4–9	14–19 EZ	1962	Bedford VAS1	UTA	B20F [1]	1973–74
10	825 EZ	1962	Bedford SB5	Duple (M)	B41F	1973
11–34	111, 12–34 FZ	1963–64	Bedford SB5	UTA	B40F	1973–74
35–59	35–59 GZ	1964	Bedford SB5	UTA	B49F	1974
60	TGB 752	1957	Albion Aberdonian MR11L	Alexander (F)	DP41F	1974
61–84	1061–84 XI	1960	Albion Aberdonian MR11L	UTA	DP41F	1974
85–117	6085–117 XI	1960	Albion Aberdonian MR11L	UTA	DP41F [2]	1974–76
118	2318 GZ	1964	Bedford VAL14	UTA	B56F	*

Fleet No	Reg No	Built	Chassis type	Body type	Seats	Wdn
119–43	119–143 GZ	1964	Bedford SB5	UTA	B49F	1974–75
144	144 GZ	1964	Bedford VAS1	UTA	C21F [3]	*
145–79	2145–79 GZ	1965	Bedford SB5	UTA/Duple	C41F	1971–74
230–33	7230–33 FZ	1963	AEC Reliance 2MU3RA	UTA	B42F	1974
234–41	6234–41 EZ	1963	AEC Reliance 2MU3RA	UTA	C41F	1979–80
243–73	6243–73 EZ	1963	AEC Reliance 2MU3RA	UTA	C41F [4]	1978–80
274–85	274–85 FZ	1963	AEC Reliance 2MU3RA	UTA	B42F	1979
285–99	6285–99 FZ	1963	AEC Reliance 2MU3RA	UTA	B42F	1977–80
300	UZ 9300	1957	Commer TS3	Beadle Integral	B43F	1968
301	PZ 4874	1954	Leyland Tiger Cub PSUC1/5T	Saro	B44F	1971
302–61	UZ 302–61	1956–57	Leyland Tiger Cub PSUC1/5T	UTA	B43F	1974–77
362–420	UZ 7362–420	1957	Leyland Tiger Cub PSUC1/5T	UTA	DP41F	1974–77
421–80	7421–80 CZ	1962	Leyland Tiger Cub PSUC1/12	UTA	C41F [5]	1977–80
481–84	2481–84 OZ	1965	Leyland Leopard PSU3/3	UTA	C42FT [6]	1976–80
485–86	2485–86 OZ	1966	Leyland Leopard PSU4/3RT	UTA	C37F [7]	1980
526–40	OCS 726–40	1965	Leyland Leopard L1	Alexander (F)	C30FT [8]	1977–78
568	GZ 6121	1947	Leyland Tiger PS1	NIRTB	B34R	1967
590–91	1015–16 AZ	1960	AEC Reliance 2MU3RV	Plaxton	C36F	1974
592–93	9592–93 AZ	1961	AEC Reliance 2MU3RV	Plaxton	C36F	1973–74
594–95	594–95 AZ	1962	AEC Reliance 2MU3RA	Plaxton	C36F	1973–74
598	IL 7077	1954	Leyland Royal Tiger PSU1/12	Burlingham Seagull	C41C	1968
599	8992 FZ	1964	Austin J2VA16	Martin Walter	C11	1968
600–660	WZ 600–660	1957–58	Leyland Titan PD2/10c	UTA	H32/28RD	1969–72
676	GZ 6156	1947	Leyland Tiger PS1/4	NIRTB	B34R	1967
681–720	UZ 681–720	1956	Leyland Titan PD2/10c	UTA	H32/28RD	1970–72
721–751	UZ 7721–51	1957	Leyland Titan PD2/10c	UTA	H32/28RD [9]	1970–72
752–777	1752–77 OI	1958	Leyland Titan PD2/10c	UTA	H32/28RD	1970–72
785–818	785–818 EZ	1962–63	Leyland Titan PD3/4	UTA	H39/30F [10]	1975–79
819–858	8819–58 AZ	1961	Leyland Titan PD3/4	UTA	H39/30F	1974–77
869–906	869–906 AZ	1960–61	Leyland Titan PD3/4	UTA	H39/30F	1973–77
916/7/9	MZ 7778/9/81	1950	Leyland Titan PD2/1	UTA	L27/26RD	1967
921/3/5	MZ 7783/5/7	1950	Leyland Titan PD2/1	UTA	L27/26RD	1967
927–33	MZ 7789–95	1950	Leyland Titan PD2/1	UTA	L27/26RD	1968
934–50	OZ 2121–37	1951–52	Leyland Titan PD2/10	UTA	L31/28RD	1968–69
951–54	PZ 5869–72	1954	Leyland Titan PD2/10	UTA	L31/28RD	1968–69
955–66	TZ 2584–95	1955	Leyland Titan PD2/10	UTA	L31/28RD	1968–69
967–85	1967–85 OI	1959	Leyland Titan PD3/4	UTA	H39/28F	1973–77
986–90	1986–90 OI	1959	Leyland Titan PD3/5	UTA	H39/28F	1975
991–96	5991–96 EZ	1963	Leyland Titan PD3/4	UTA	H39/30F	1975–78
7845	GZ 6073	1947	Leyland Tiger PS1	NIRTB	B32F	1968
8600	GZ 7668	1948	Leyland Tiger PS1	NIRTB	B34R	1967
8858	MZ 1929	1949	Leyland Tiger PS2/1	UTA	B37F	1969
8930–31	MZ 7965–66	1951	Leyland Royal Tiger PSU1/11	UTA	B42F	1967/71
8932–36	MZ 7967–71	1951	Leyland Royal Tiger PSU1/11	UTA	B42F	1970–72
8938/42	MZ 7973/75	1951	Leyland Royal Tiger PSU1/11	UTA	B42F	1970–72
8943–45	MZ 9883–85	1951	Leyland Royal Tiger PSU1/11	UTA	B42F	1969–72
8946–57	OZ 819–30	1951	Leyland Royal Tiger PSU1/11	UTA	B42F	1969–71
8958–82	OZ 831–55	1953	Leyland Royal Tiger PSU1/11	UTA	B42F	1968–72
8984/6–94	OZ 837/9–67	1953	Leyland Royal Tiger PSU1/11	UTA	B42F	1970–71
8995–96	IL 5605, 5898	1951–52	Leyland Royal Tiger PSU1/9	Saro	B44F	1969–70
9000–12	ECK xxx	1952	Leyland Royal Tiger PSU1/13	Leyland	B44F	1970–73
9013–37	ERN xxx	1952	Leyland Royal Tiger PSU1/13	Leyland	B44F	1970–73
9100–06	DRN xxx	1951	Leyland Olympic HR40	Weymann	B44F	1970–71
9301–50 [11]	SWS 1–50	1959	Leyland Tiger Cub PSU1/3	MCW	B44F [12]	1974–75

[1] Nos 4–9 reseated B28F 1967

[2] Nos 86, 94 were C37F

[3] No 144 reseated B28F 1967

[4] Nos 264/5 were C36F; No 268 was C37FT and reseated C41F in 1969.

[5] Nos 440/55/64 were C37F; No 455 was reseated C41F.

[6] All reseated C45F by 1969; No 481 reseated B64F in 1974.

[7] No 486 reseated B43F in 1975.

[8] No 526 reseated C37F in 1967; Nos 533/7 reseated C38F in 1967; remainder reseated C36F in 1967. All except 533/6 reseated B41F in 1970–71; No 536 reseated B39F in 1970.

[9] No 721 rebodied in 1967 using body ex No 703.

[10] Nos 791–94 were H38/26F.

[11] Batch excluding 9309/22. Batch renumbered 1001–50 in Jan 1969.

[12] No 9326 was B47F, later reduced to B46F; all others reduced to B43F.

Withdrawal dates of inherited vehicles

Fleet No	Regist No	Withdrawn	Fleet No	Regist No	Withdrawn	Fleet No	Regist No	Withdrawn	Fleet No	Regist No	Withdrawn	Fleet No	Regist No	Withdrawn
1	8813 AZ	1969s	50	50 GZ	1974	99	6099 XI	1971m	148	2148 MZ	1971s	247	6247 EZ	1971m
2	8814 AZ	1969s	51	51 GZ	1975	100	6100 XI	1971m	149	2149 MZ	1972s	248	6248 EZ	1979
3	8815 AZ	1968s	52	52 GZ	1969m	101	6101 XI	1975	150	2150 MZ	1973s	249	6249 EZ	1971m
4	14 EZ	1973s	53	53 GZ	1971m	102	6102 XI	1973	151	2151 MZ	1974s	250	6250 EZ	1979
5	15 EZ	1973s	54	54 GZ	1973s	103	6103 XI	1974	152	2152 MZ	1974s	251	6251 EZ	1980
6	16 EZ	1974s	55	55 GZ	1973	104	6104 XI	1972m	153	2153 MZ	1973s	252	6252 EZ	1978
7	17 EZ	1972m	56	56 GZ	1972m	105	6105 XI	1974	154	2154 MZ	1971s	253	6253 EZ	1979
8	18 EZ	1972m	57	57 GZ	1972m	106	6106 XI	1976	155	2155 MZ	1972m	254	6254 EZ	1972m
9	19 EZ	1974s	58	58 GZ	1971m	107	6107 XI	1972m	156	2156 MZ	1971s	255	6255 EZ	1969m
10	825 EZ	1973s	59	59 GZ	1971m	108	6108 XI	1973	157	2157 MZ	1972s	256	6256 EZ	1979
11	111 FZ	1972f	60	TGB 752	1974	109	6109 XI	1969m	158	2158 MZ	1973s	257	6257 EZ	1979
12	12 FZ	1973	61	1061 XI	1974m	110	6110 XI	1974	159	2159 MZ	1972s	258	6258 EZ	1972m
13	13 FZ	1973	62	1062 XI	1972m	111	6111 XI	1975	160	2160 MZ	1972s	259	6259 EZ	1977m
14	14 FZ	1973	63	1063 XI	1975	112	6112 XI	1973m	161	2161 MZ	1971s	260	6260 EZ	1979
15	15 FZ	1973s	64	1064 XI	1969m	113	6113 XI	1976	162	2162 MZ	1972s	261	6261 EZ	1971m
16	16 FZ	1974s	65	1065 XI	1974	114	6114 XI	1974	163	2163 MZ	1973s	262	6262 EZ	1979
17	17 FZ	1972m	66	1066 XI	1974	115	6115 XI	1974	164	2164 MZ	1973s	263	6263 EZ	1976m
18	18 FZ	1974s	67	1067 XI	1975	116	6116 XI	1974	165	2165 MZ	1973s	264	6264 EZ	1972m
19	19 FZ	1972m	68	1068 XI	1974	117	6117 XI	1975	166	2166 MZ	1973s	265	6265 EZ	1978
20	20 FZ	1973a	69	1069 XI	1974	118	2318 GZ	1973m	167	2167 MZ	1975s	266	6266 EZ	1978a
21	21 FZ	1971m	70	1070 XI	1975	119	119 GZ	1974s	168	2168 MZ	1973s	267	6267 EZ	1976m
22	22 FZ	1972m	71	1071 XI	1974	120	120 GZ	1974	169	2169 MZ	1974s	268	6268 EZ	1980m
23	23 FZ	1973	72	1072 XI	1974	121	121 GZ	1974	170	2170 MZ	1974s	269	6269 EZ	1976m
24	24 FZ	1973	73	1073 XI	1974	122	122 GZ	1974	171	2171 MZ	1973s	270	6270 EZ	1974m
25	25 FZ	1972a	74	1074 XI	1975	123	123 GZ	1971m	172	2172 MZ	1973s	271	6271 EZ	1979
26	26 FZ	1972m	75	1075 XI	1972m	124	124 GZ	1974	173	2173 MZ	1974	272	6272 EZ	1967a
27	27 FZ	1973s	76	1076 XI	1975	125	125 GZ	1973m	174	2174 MZ	1975s	273	6273 EZ	1974m
28	28 FZ	1974	77	1077 XI	1973	126	126 GZ	1975s	175	2175 MZ	1971s	274	274 FZ	1971m
29	29 FZ	1974	78	1078 XI	1973	127	127 GZ	1974	176	2176 MZ	1971s	275	275 FZ	1972m
30	30 FZ	1973s	79	1079 XI	1974m	128	128 GZ	1974s	177	2177 MZ	1971s	276	276 FZ	1972m
31	31 FZ	1973s	80	1080 XI	1973a	129	129 GZ	1974	178	2178 MZ	1971s	277	277 FZ	1978m
32	32 FZ	1969m	81	1081 XI	1975	130	130 GZ	1973	179	2179 MZ	1971s	278	278 FZ	1971m
33	33 FZ	1974f	82	1082 XI	1974	131	131 GZ	1975				279	279 FZ	1979
34	34 FZ	1974s	83	1083 XI	1969m	132	132 GZ	1974	230	7230 FZ	1974a	280	280 FZ	1974m
35	35 GZ	1971m	84	1084 XI	1974m	133	133 GZ	1974s	231	7231 FZ	1970m	281	281 FZ	1979
36	36 GZ	1974	85	6085 XI	1974	134	134 GZ	1974s	232	7232 FZ	1971m	282	282 FZ	1978m
37	37 GZ	1974	86	6086 XI	1975	135	135 GZ	1972m	233	7233 FZ	1974m	283	283 FZ	1972m
38	38 GZ	1974s	87	6087 XI	1973	136	136 GZ	1973s	234	6234 EZ	1980p	284	284 FZ	1979
39	39 GZ	1974	88	6088 XI	1976	137	137 GZ	1972m	235	6235 EZ	1980	285	285 FZ	1978m
40	40 GZ	1974s	89	6089 XI	1974	138	138 GZ	1974	236	6236 EZ	1980	286	6286 FZ	1977
41	41 GZ	1974s	90	6090 XI	1971m	139	139 GZ	1974	237	6237 EZ	1979	287	6287 FZ	1978m
42	42 GZ	1971m	91	6091 XI	1974	140	140 GZ	1975	238	6238 EZ	1978m	288	6288 FZ	1972m
43	43 GZ	1972m	92	6092 XI	1975s	141	141 GZ	1973m	239	6239 EZ	1972m	289	6289 FZ	1978m
44	44 GZ	1974s	93	6093 XI	1967a	142	142 GZ	1974	240	6240 EZ	1978a	290	6290 FZ	1974m
45	45 GZ	1972m	94	6094 XI	1974	143	143 GZ	1974s	241	6241 EZ	1979	291	6291 FZ	1978r
46	46 GZ	1974	95	6095 XI	1974	144	144 GZ	1972m	243	6243 EZ	1980	292	6292 FZ	1978m
47	47 GZ	1974s	96	6096 XI	1974	145	2145 MZ	1971s	244	6244 EZ	1979	293	6293 FZ	1974m
48	48 GZ	1971m	97	6097 XI	1974	146	2146 MZ	1971s	245	6245 EZ	1980	294	6294 FZ	1978m
49	49 GZ	1973	98	6098 XI	1975	147	2147 MZ	1971s	246	6246 EZ	1979s	295	6295 FZ	1980

Fleet No	Regist No	With-drawn	Fleet No	Regist No	With-drawn	Fleet No	Regist No	With-drawn	Fleet No	Regist No	With-drawn	Fleet No	Regist No	With-drawn
296	6296 FZ	1978	359	UZ 359	1976a	422	7422 CZ	1980s	485	2485 OZ	1974m	633	WZ 633	1972m
297	6297 FZ	1970m	360	UZ 360	1972m	423	7423 CZ	1975m	486	2486 OZ	1980r	634	WZ 634	1971
298	6298 FZ	1974m	361	UZ 361	1972m	424	7424 CZ	1979s				635	WZ 635	1972s
299	6299 FZ	1974m	362	UZ 7362	1972m	425	7425 CZ	1977s	526	OCS 726	1974m	636	WZ 636	1972m
300	UZ 9300	1968	363	UZ 7363	1972m	426	7426 CZ	1974m	527	OCS 727	1978r	637	WZ 637	1972s
301	PZ 4874	1971p	364	UZ 7364	1972m	427	7427 CZ	1980r	528	OCS 728	1971m	638	WZ 638	1972s
302	UZ 302	1977s	365	UZ 7365	1974a	428	7428 CZ	1980r	529	OCS 729	1979r	639	WZ 639	1971
303	UZ 303	1974	366	UZ 7366	1976m	429	7429 CZ	1974m	530	OCS 730	1977r	640	WZ 640	1972m
304	UZ 304	1977	367	UZ 7367	1973t	430	7430 CZ	1971m	531	OCS 731	1978r	641	WZ 641	1972s
305	UZ 305	1977s	368	UZ 7368	1976	431	7431 CZ	1972m	532	OCS 732	1974m	642	WZ 642	1972t
306	UZ 306	1977	369	UZ 7369	1974	432	7432 CZ	1977s	533	OCS 733	1977r	643	WZ 643	1972
307	UZ 307	1971m	370	UZ 7370	1977s	433	7433 CZ	1977	534	OCS 734	1978r	644	WZ 644	1972s
308	UZ 308	1976u	371	UZ 7371	1971m	434	7434 CZ	1980s	535	OCS 735	1977r	645	WZ 645	1971s
309	UZ 309	1977u	372	UZ 7372	1977r	435	7435 CZ	1971m	536	OCS 736	1973a	646	WZ 646	1972t
310	UZ 310	1972m	373	UZ 7373	1977	436	7436 CZ	1976m	537	OCS 737	1977r	647	WZ 647	1972
311	UZ 311	1977	374	UZ 7374	1976m	437	7437 CZ	1979s	538	OCS 738	1978r	648	WZ 648	1971s
312	UZ 312	1974	375	UZ 7375	1976	438	7438 CZ	1979	539	OCS 739	1972m	649	WZ 649	1971
313	UZ 313	1971m	376	UZ 7376	1977u	439	7439 CZ	1980s	540	OCS 740	1980r	650	WZ 650	1969t
314	UZ 314	1971m	377	UZ 7377	1975	440	7440 CZ	1979u				651	WZ 651	1972m
315	UZ 315	1971m	378	UZ 7378	1977	441	7441 CZ	1980	568	GZ 6121	1967	652	WZ 652	1969t
316	UZ 316	1971m	379	UZ 7379	1977	442	7442 CZ	1979r				653	WZ 653	1971
317	UZ 317	1976s	380	UZ 7380	1971m	443	7443 CZ	1979	590	1015 AZ	1974	654	WZ 654	1971
318	UZ 318	1977p	381	UZ 7381	1974	444	7444 CZ	1979	591	1016 AZ	1974	655	WZ 655	1971
319	UZ 319	1977m	382	UZ 7382	1976s	445	7445 CZ	1976m	592	9592 AZ	1974s	656	WZ 656	1972
320	UZ 320	1977	383	UZ 7383	1977	446	7446 CZ	1977	593	9593 AZ	1973	657	WZ 657	1972a
321	UZ 321	1977r	384	UZ 7384	1974	447	7447 CZ	1976m	594	494 EZ	1974s	658	WZ 658	1972
322	UZ 322	1977	385	UZ 7385	1977	448	7448 CZ	1976m	595	495 EZ	1973	659	WZ 659	1971p
323	UZ 323	1977	386	UZ 7386	1975	449	7449 CZ	1976m				660	WZ 660	1971s
324	UZ 324	1976s	387	UZ 7387	1974	450	7450 CZ	1971m	598	IL 7077	1968			
325	UZ 325	1977	388	UZ 7388	1975	451	7451 CZ	1979s	599	8990 FZ	1968	676	GZ 6156	1967
326	UZ 326	1978	389	UZ 7389	1972m	452	7452 CZ	1971m	600	WZ 600	1972m			
327	UZ 327	1978	390	UZ 7390	1976m	453	7453 CZ	1979r	601	WZ 601	1972	681	UZ 681	1971
328	UZ 328	1977	391	UZ 7391	1969m	454	7454 CZ	1980u	602	WZ 602	1971	682	UZ 682	1970t
329	UZ 329	1977r	392	UZ 7392	1977	455	7455 CZ	1976m	603	WZ 603	1970	683	UZ 683	1971
330	UZ 330	1976t	393	UZ 7393	1975	456	7456 CZ	1976m	604	WZ 604	1972	684	UZ 684	1972
331	UZ 331	1968a	394	UZ 7394	1974	457	7457 CZ	1971m	605	WZ 605	1972	685	UZ 685	1971
332	UZ 332	1977r	395	UZ 7395	1977s	458	7458 CZ	1980r	606	WZ 606	1972t	686	UZ 686	1972
333	UZ 333	1972a	396	UZ 7396	1976	459	7459 CZ	1977a	607	WZ 607	1972	687	UZ 687	1972t
334	UZ 334	1976	397	UZ 7397	1972m	460	7460 CZ	1976m	608	WZ 608	1971	688	UZ 688	1972
335	UZ 335	1976m	398	UZ 7398	1972m	461	7461 CZ	1971m	609	WZ 609	1970	689	UZ 689	1972m
336	UZ 336	1971m	399	UZ 7399	1975	462	7462 CZ	1980s	610	WZ 610	1970	690	UZ 690	1972
337	UZ 337	1973a	400	UZ 7400	1973m	463	7463 CZ	1971m	611	WZ 611	1972s	691	UZ 691	1972
338	UZ 338	1977	401	UZ 7401	1976m	464	7464 CZ	1972m	612	WZ 612	1970a	692	UZ 692	1971
339	UZ 339	1977	402	UZ 7402	1975	465	7465 CZ	1977m	613	WZ 613	1971	693	UZ 693	1972
340	UZ 340	1977s	403	UZ 7403	1976m	466	7466 CZ	1979	614	WZ 614	1972	694	UZ 694	1972
341	UZ 341	1974	404	UZ 7404	1974f	467	7467 CZ	1977	615	WZ 615	1972	695	UZ 695	1971
342	UZ 342	1977a	405	UZ 7405	1975	468	7468 CZ	1979r	616	WZ 616	1970	696	UZ 696	1971m
343	UZ 343	1975	406	UZ 7406	1978m	469	7469 CZ	1972m	617	WZ 617	1971	697	UZ 697	1971s
344	UZ 344	1977	407	UZ 7407	1977	470	7470 CZ	1971m	618	WZ 618	1972	698	UZ 698	1971
345	UZ 345	1974	408	UZ 7408	1977	471	7471 CZ	1969m	619	WZ 619	1971	699	UZ 699	1972
346	UZ 346	1976s	409	UZ 7409	1976m	472	7472 CZ	1976m	620	WZ 620	1972t	700	UZ 700	1971
347	UZ 347	1976m	410	UZ 7410	1975	473	7473 CZ	1980	621	WZ 621	1972m	701	UZ 701	1971
348	UZ 348	1977t	411	UZ 7411	1977m	474	7474 CZ	1980s	622	WZ 622	1972	702	UZ 702	1971
349	UZ 349	1977	412	UZ 7412	1977s	475	7475 CZ	1971p	623	WZ 623	1971	703	UZ 703*	1966a
350	UZ 350	1975	413	UZ 7413	1976	476	7476 CZ	1979	624	WZ 624	1972	704	UZ 704	1971
351	UZ 351	1975	414	UZ 7414	1976	477	7477 CZ	1969m	625	WZ 625	1971s	705	UZ 705	1970a
352	UZ 352	1976m	415	UZ 7415	1975	478	7478 CZ	1979	626	WZ 626	1972s	706	UZ 706	1969t
353	UZ 353	1975	416	UZ 7416	1977	479	7479 CZ	1971m	627	WZ 627	1971s	707	UZ 707	1972
354	UZ 354	1976	417	UZ 7417	1972m	480	7480 CZ	1980r	628	WZ 628	1971	708	UZ 708	1971
355	UZ 355	1973m	418	UZ 7418	1972m	481	2481 OZ	1980s	629	WZ 629	1971	709	UZ 709	1972
356	UZ 356	1974	419	UZ 7419	1971m	482	2482 OZ	1976s	630	WZ 630	1972	710	UZ 710	1971
357	UZ 357	1977	420	UZ 7420	1972m	483	2483 OZ	1976s	631	WZ 631	1971	711	UZ 711	1969
358	UZ 358	1975	421	7421 CZ	1980	484	2484 OZ	1972m	632	WZ 632	1972	712	UZ 712	1972

* No 703 was damaged and inactive but still in the official list; its body was reused in 1967 on No 721 (Note 9, page 175).

Fleet No	Regist No	Withdrawn	Fleet No	Regist No	Withdrawn	Fleet No	Regist No	Withdrawn	Fleet No	Regist No	Withdrawn	Fleet No	Regist No	Withdrawn
713	UZ 713	1970	776	1776 OI	1972m	845	8845 AZ	1977	930	MZ 7792	1969	993	5993 EZ	1972m
714	UZ 714	1971	777	1777 OI	1972	846	8846 AZ	1980t	931	MZ 7793	1969	994	5994 EZ	1979t
715	UZ 715	1970				847	8847 AZ	1975	932	MZ 7794	1967	995	5995 EZ	1975
716	UZ 716	1969t	785	785 EZ	1976	848	8848 AZ	1971m	933	MZ 7795	1968	996	5996 EZ	1975
717	UZ 717	1971	786	786 EZ	1975	849	8849 AZ	1978t	934	OZ 2121	1967			
718	UZ 718	1972	787	787 EZ	1974m	850	8850 AZ	1972m	935	OZ 2122	1968	1001	SWS 1	1974c
719	UZ 719	1971	788	788 EZ	1975s	851	8851 AZ	1975s	936	OZ 2123	1968	1002	SWS 2	1972a
720	UZ 720	1972	789	789 EZ	1976	852	8852 AZ	1978t	937	OZ 2124	1967	1003	SWS 3	1974c
721	UZ 7721	1971	790	790 EZ	1979	853	8853 AZ	1974	938	OZ 2125	1969	1004	SWS 4	1974
722	UZ 7722	1971	791	791 EZ	1975s	854	8854 AZ	1975	939	OZ 2126	1968	1005	SWS 5	1976c
723	UZ 7723	1972m	792	792 EZ	1975	855	8855 AZ	1976	940	OZ 2127	1969	1006	SWS 6	1976
724	UZ 7724	1972	793	793 EZ	1976s	856	8856 AZ	1972	941	OZ 2128	1967	1007	SWS 7	1974
725	UZ 7725	1972m	794	794 EZ	1972a	857	8857 AZ	1973m	942	OZ 2129	1967s	1008	SWS 8	1974c
726	UZ 7726	1971	795	795 EZ	1977	858	8858 AZ	1975s	943	OZ 2130	1969	1010	SWS 10	1974c
727	UZ 7727	1972	796	796 EZ	1975				944	OZ 2131	1969	1011	SWS 11	1976c
728	UZ 7728	1972m	797	797 EZ	1975m	869	869 AZ	1973	945	OZ 2132	1968	1012	SWS 12	1974c
729	UZ 7729	1972	798	798 EZ	1979ut	870	870 AZ	1978t	946	OZ 2133	1967	1013	SWS 13	1975
730	UZ 7730	1972m	799	799 EZ	1978t	871	871 AZ	1977	947	OZ 2134	1969	1014	SWS 14	1974
731	UZ 7731	1971s	800	800 EZ	1974m	872	872 AZ	1976	948	OZ 2135	1969	1015	SWS 15	1974c
732	UZ 7732	1971	801	801 EZ	1978t	873	873 AZ	1973	949	OZ 2136	1969	1016	SWS 16	1972m
733	UZ 7733	1972	802	802 EZ	1975s	874	874 AZ	1975u	950	OZ 2137	1968	1017	SWS 17	1974c
734	UZ 7734	1969t	803	803 EZ	1974m	875	875 AZ	1972m	951	PZ 5869	1969	1018	SWS 18	1974c
735	UZ 7735	1971	804	804 EZ	1975	876	876 AZ	1977t	952	PZ 5870	1968	1019	SWS 19	1975c
736	UZ 7736	1971	805	805 EZ	1975	877	877 AZ	1976s	953	PZ 5871	1968	1020	SWS 20	1975
737	UZ 7737	1971	806	806 EZ	1973m	878	878 AZ	1976	954	PZ 5872	1969	1021	SWS 21	1974
738	UZ 7738	1972m	807	807 EZ	1979	879	879 AZ	1975	955	TZ 2585	1969	1023	SWS 23	1975c
739	UZ 7739	1971	808	808 EZ	1974m	880	880 AZ	1972m	956	TZ 2586	1970	1024	SWS 24	1974c
740	UZ 7740	1971	809	809 EZ	1978t	881	881 AZ	1974m	957	TZ 2587	1969	1025	SWS 25	1974c
741	UZ 7741	1975	810	810 EZ	1977s	882	882 AZ	1974m	958	TZ 2588	1969	1026	SWS 26	1975c
742	UZ 7742	1971	811	811 EZ	1975	883	883 AZ	1973m	959	TZ 2589	1968	1027	SWS 27	1974
743	UZ 7743	1970	812	812 EZ	1975	884	884 AZ	1975	960	TZ 2590	1969	1028	SWS 28	1976c
744	UZ 7744	1971	813	813 EZ	1975	885	885 AZ	1974	961	TZ 2590	1969	1029	SWS 29	1974c
745	UZ 7745	1971s	814	814 EZ	1972m	886	886 AZ	1977	962	TZ 2591	1969	1030	SWS 30	1974c
746	UZ 7746	1971	815	815 EZ	1977tp	887	887 AZ	1976	963	TZ 2592	1969	1031	SWS 31	1977c
747	UZ 7747	1970	816	816 EZ	1974m	888	888 AZ	1972a	964	TZ 2593	1969	1032	SWS 32	1974c
748	UZ 7748	1971	817	817 EZ	1975	889	889 AZ	1973m	965	TZ 2594	1968	1033	SWS 33	1974c
749	UZ 7749	1971	818	818 EZ	1975	890	890 AZ	1975	966	TZ 2595	1968	1034	SWS 34	1974c
750	UZ 7750	1971	819	8819 AZ	1975t	891	891 AZ	1976	967	1967 OI	1973t	1035	SWS 35	1975c
751	UZ 7751	1972m	820	8820 AZ	1973m	892	892 AZ	1977s	968	1968 OI	1971m	1036	SWS 36	1972m
752	1752 OI	1971	821	8821 AZ	1980	893	893 AZ	1975s	969	1969 OI	1971a	1037	SWS 37	1974c
753	1753 OI	1971	822	8822 AZ	1973a	894	894 AZ	1975	970	1970 OI	1977	1038	SWS 38	1974c
754	1754 OI	1972s	823	8823 AZ	1976	895	895 AZ	1977s	971	1971 OI	1972m	1039	SWS 39	1976uc
755	1755 OI	1972m	824	8824 AZ	1975t	896	896 AZ	1973m	972	1972 OI	1972a	1040	SWS 40	1974c
756	1756 OI	1971	825	8825 AZ	1977	897	897 AZ	1972a	973	1973 OI	1972m	1041	SWS 41	1974c
757	1757 OI	1971	826	8826 AZ	1974t	898	898 AZ	1976	974	1974 OI	1973t	1042	SWS 42	1974c
758	1758 OI	1971	827	8827 AZ	1974m	899	899 AZ	1975t	975	1975 OI	1973t	1043	SWS 43	1974c
759	1759 OI	1971s	828	8828 AZ	1976s	900	900 AZ	1971m	976	1976 OI	1973	1044	SWS 44	1975c
760	1760 OI	1971	829	8829 AZ	1973t	901	901 AZ	1971m	977	1977 OI	1973	1045	SWS 45	1975c
761	1761 OI	1971	830	8830 AZ	1977	902	902 AZ	1975	978	1978 OI	1972m	1046	SWS 46	1974c
762	1762 OI	1971	831	8831 AZ	1972m	903	903 AZ	1973	979	1979 OI	1974m	1047	SWS 47	1971m
763	1763 OI	1970s	832	8832 AZ	1972m	904	904 AZ	1971m	980	1980 OI	1972	1048	SWS 48	1974
764	1764 OI	1971	833	8833 AZ	1975s	905	905 AZ	1975s	981	1981 OI	1977	1049	SWS 49	1970
765	1765 OI	1971	834	8834 AZ	1977	906	906 AZ	1975	982	1982 OI	1977s	1050	SWS 50	1975c
766	1766 OI	1971	835	8835 AZ	1976				983	1983 OI	1976			
767	1767 OI	1971s	836	8836 AZ	1975s	916	MZ 7778	1967	984	1984 OI	1973m	7845	GZ 6073	1968t
768	1768 OI	1971s	837	8837 AZ	1975	917	MZ 7779	1967	985	1985 OI	1976	8600	GZ 7668	1967s
769	1769 OI	1971	838	8838 AZ	1977s	919	MZ 7781	1968	986	1986 OI	1972m			
770	1770 OI	1971	839	8839 AZ	1978	921	MZ 7783	1967	987	1987 OI	1975c	8858	MZ 1929	1969tp
771	1771 OI	1971	840	8840 AZ	1975	923	MZ 7785	1967	988	1988 OI	1971m	8930	MZ 7965	1967
772	1772 OI	1972s	841	8841 AZ	1977	925	MZ 7787	1967	989	1989 OI	1975c	8931	MZ 7966	1971
773	1773 OI	1972	842	8842 AZ	1977	927	MZ 7789	1969p	990	1990 OI	1973t	8932	MZ 7967	1970
774	1774 OI	1972	843	8843 AZ	1977s	928	MZ 7790	1967	991	5991 EZ	1978	8933	MZ 7968	1971s
775	1775 OI	1972	844	8844 AZ	1972m	929	MZ 7791	1968	992	5992 EZ	1976	8934	MZ 7969	1969

Fleet No	Regist No	Withdrawn
8935	MZ 7970	1972
8936	MZ 7971	1971
8938	MZ 7973	1972
8942	MZ 7975	1970
8943	MZ 9883	1972
8944	MZ 9884	1969
8945	MZ 9885	1971
8946	OZ 819	1969
8947	OZ 820	1970
8948	OZ 821	1970
8949	OZ 822	1968
8950	OZ 823	1969
8951	OZ 824	1972
8952	OZ 825	1970
8953	OZ 826	1970s
8954	OZ 827	1971
8955	OZ 828	1971
8956	OZ 829	1969
8957	OZ 830	1970
8958	OZ 831	1971
8959	OZ 832	1971
8960	OZ 833	1970f
8961	OZ 834	1971
8962	OZ 835	1969
8963	OZ 836	1972r
8964	OZ 837	1969s
8965	OZ 838	1969
8966	OZ 839	1971
8967	OZ 840	1968
8968	OZ 841	1971
8969	OZ 842	1971
8970	OZ 843	1971
8971	OZ 844	1972m
8972	OZ 845	1969m
8973	OZ 846	1971
8974	OZ 847	1971
8975	OZ 848	1971s
8976	OZ 849	1971
8977	OZ 850	1972
8978	OZ 851	1968
8979	OZ 852	1971s
8980	OZ 853	1970
8981	OZ 854	1969
8982	OZ 855	1971
8984	OZ 857	1971
8986	OZ 859	1971
8987	OZ 860	1971s
8988	OZ 861	1971
8989	OZ 862	1970
8990	OZ 863	1970
8991	OZ 864	1971
8992	OZ 865	1969
8993	OZ 866	1970
8994	OZ 867	1972
8995	IL 5605	1970
8996	IL 5898	1969
9000	ECK 562	1971m
9001	ECK 563	1971
9002	ECK 565	1969m
9003	ECK 569	1970
9004	ECK 574	1970
9005	ECK 581	1972r
9006	ECK 593	1971s
9007	ECK 594	1970r
9008	ECK 595	1974r
9009	ECK 596	1967a
9010	ECK 600	1973r
9011	ECK 603	1971r
9012	ECK 611	1971
9013	ERN 684	1973r
9014	ERN 688	1973r
9015	ERN 690	1972
9016	ERN 694	1973
9017	ERN 695	1971
9018	ERN 697	1971r
9019	ERN 698	1970
9020	ERN 699	1973
9021	ERN 701	1970
9022	ERN 702	1970
9023	ERN 703	1970
9024	ERN 704	1972
9025	ERN 705	1972m
9026	ERN 706	1973
9027	ERN 708	1973r
9028	ERN 709	1971r
9029	ERN 710	1970
9030	ERN 711	1971
9031	ERN 712	1969m
9032	ERN 713	1971r
9033	ERN 715	1971r
9034	ERN 721	1971
9035	ERN 722	1969m
9036	ERN 723	1971r
9037	ERN 725	1971r
9100	DRN 114	1971
9101	DRN 115	1971
9102	DRN 116	1970
9103	DRN 125	1971r
9104	DRN 127	1971r
9105	DRN 130	1971
9106	DRN 134	1969m

(2) Vehicles built new for Ulsterbus 1967–1988

Fleet No	Reg No	Built	Chassis type	Body type	Seats	Wdn
487–93	487–93 TZ	1967	Leyland Leopard PSU3/3RT	Potter/Alexander 'Y'	C44F	1980
584–89	584–89 TZ	1967	Leyland Leopard PSU/3	Plaxton Panorama	C41F	1980
[1] 9201–70	1201–70 TZ	1967	Bedford VAM14	Duple (N)	DP45F	1978–80
494–98	4494–98 UZ	1968–69	Leyland Leopard PSU3A/4RT	Potter	C49F	1981
1101–10	4101–10 UZ	1968	Bristol LH6L	Potter	DP41F	1980
1051–70	9051–70 UZ	1969	Bristol RELL6L	Alexander (F) /Potter	B44D	1985
1301–20	4001–20 WZ	1969	Leyland Leopard PSU3A/4R	Potter	B53F	1984–88
1321–40	4021–40 WZ	1969	Leyland Leopard PSU3A/4R	Potter	DP49F	1984–86
1341–50	AOI 1341–50	1969	Leyland Leopard PSU3A/4R	Alexander (B)	DP49F	1985
1351–71	BOI 1351–71	1970	Leyland Leopard PSU3A/4R	Alexander (B)	DP49F	1984–86
1372	BOI 1372	1970	Leyland Leopard PSU3A/4R	Alexander (B)	C49F [2]	*
1373–400	BOI 1373–400	1970–71	Leyland Leopard PSU3A/4R	Alexander (B)	DP49F	1985–87
501–10	BOI 1501–10	1970	Leyland Leopard PSU3A/4RT	Alexander (B)	C49F	1985
1401–16	BOI 1401–16	1971	Leyland Leopard PSU3A/4R	Alexander (B)	B53F	1986–88
578–83	COI 578–83	1971	Leyland Leopard PSU3A/4R	Plaxton Elite	C49F	1983–84
511–20	COI 511–20	1971	Leyland Leopard PSU3A/4RT	Alexander (B)	C49F	1984–85
911–21/3	COI 911–21/3	1971	Leyland Atlantean PDR2/1	Alexander (B)	H48/37F [3]	1986–90
1417–50	COI 1417–50	1971	Leyland Leopard PSU3A/4R	Alexander (B)	B53F	1986–87
1451–500	DOI 3451–500	1971–72	Leyland Leopard PSU3B/4R	Alexander (B)	DP49F	1985–88
1501–50	DOI 1501–50	1972	Leyland Leopard PSU3B/4R	Alexander (B)	B53F	1986–88
1551–90	DOI 1551–90	1972–73	Leyland Leopard PSU3B/4R	Alexander (B)	B53F	1987–88
922/4–50	COI 922/4–50	1972–73	Leyland Atlantean PDR2/1	Alexander (B)	H48/37F [3/4]	1986–89
1601–700	FOI 1601–700	1973–74	Bristol LH6L	Alexander (B)	B45F	1981–88
1801–25	GOI 1801–25	1974	Bedford YRT	Alexander (B)	B53F	1981–83
1701–02	HOI 1701–02	1974	Bedford YRQ	Duple Dominant I	C41F	1980
1703–99	HOI 1703–99	1974	Bedford YRQ	Alexander (B)	B45F	1982–89
1800	HOI 800	1975	Bedford YRQ	Alexander (B)	B45F	1989
1901–08	HOI 1901–08	1975	Leyland Leopard PSU3C/4R	Alexander (B)	C49F	1989
1909–10	HOI 1909–10	1975	Leyland Leopard PSU3C/4R	Duple Dominant I	C49F	1985–86
1911–12	HOI 1911–12	1974	Leyland Leopard PSU3C/4R	Duple Dominant I	C49F	1986

Fleet No	Reg No	Built	Chassis type	Body type	Seats	Wdn
1913–35	HOI 2913–35	1975	Leyland Leopard PSU3C/4R	Alexander (B)	DP49F	1989–90
2001–28	JOI 3001–28	1975	Bristol RELL6G	Alexander (B)	B44D	1989–90
2029–40	JOI 3029–40	1975	Bristol RELL6G	Alexander (B)	B50F	1989–90
1936–65	KOI 9936–65	1976	Leyland Leopard PSU3C/4R	Alexander (B)	DP49F	1990–91
1831–32	LOI 1831–32	1976	Bedford YLQ	Duple Dominant I	C41F [5]	1985–86
1833–80	LOI 1833–80	1976–77	Bedford YLQ	Alexander (B)	B45F	1987–89
2121–35	MOI 2121–35	1976–77	Bristol RELL6G	Alexander (B)	B44D	1991
1966–89	NOI 1966–89	1977	Leyland Leopard PSU3D/4R [6]	Alexander (B)	DP49F	1990–94
1990–95	NOI 1990–95	1977	Leyland Leopard PSU3E/4R	Duple Dominant II	C49F	1991–92
2171–210	POI 2171–210	1977–78	Bristol RELL6G	Alexander (B)	B52F	1989–97
1830	POI 9830	1978	Bedford YLQ	Duple Dominant II	C41F	1980
101–04	ROI 101–04	1978	Leyland Leopard PSU3E/4R	Duple Dominant I	C53F	1986
105–50	ROI 105–50	1978	Leyland Leopard PSU3E/4R	Alexander (B)	DP49F	1997–2000
2231–70	ROI 2231–70	1978–79	Bristol RELL6G	Alexander (B)	B52F	1998–2000
1591	SOI 3591	1978	Leyland Leopard PSU3A/4R	Alexander (B)	B53F	1989
1664	SOI 6664	1979	Bristol LH6L	Alexander (B)	B45F	1988
151–56	TOI 151–56	1979	Leyland Leopard PSU3E/4R	Duple Dominant I	C53F	1987
1996–99	TOI 1996–99	1979	Leyland Leopard PSU3E/4R	Duple Dominant II	C49F	1992
2271–305	TOI 2271–305	1979	Bristol RELL6G	Alexander (B)	B52F	1999–2000
1592	TOI 3592	1979	Leyland Leopard PSU3A/4R	Alexander (B)	B53F	*
2361–400	UOI 2271–305	1979–80	Bristol RELL6G	Alexander (B)	B52F	1999–2000
157–70	UOI 9157–70	1980	Leyland Leopard PSU3E/4R	Alexander (B)	DP49F	–
171–206	VOI 171–206	1980	Leyland Leopard PSU3E/4R	Alexander (B)	DP49F	2000–
2431–80	WOI 2431–80	1980–81	Bristol RELL6G	Alexander (B)	B52F	1999–
207–26	WOI 2207–26	1981	Leyland Leopard PSU3E/4R	Alexander (B)	B53F	–
227–56	WOI 2227–56	1981	Leyland Leopard PSU3E/4R	Alexander (B)	DP49F	–
557–60	WOI 2557–60	1981	Leyland Leopard PSU3E/4R	Plaxton Supreme	C53F	1995
3001/5	WOI 3001/5	1981	Leyland B21	Alexander (B)	B53F	1991
561–64	XOI 561–64	1981	Leyland Leopard PSU3E/4R	Plaxton Supreme	C49F	1993
300–09	XOI 2300–09	1981	Leyland Leopard PSU3E/4R	Alexander (B)	B53F	–
3000	WOI 607	1982	Leyland B21	Alexander (B)	B45D	1991
258	XOI 2258	1982	Leyland Leopard PSU3E/4R	Wright TT	DP53F	–
260–79	YOI 2260–79	1982	Leyland Leopard PSU3G/4R	Alexander (B)	DP49F	–
280–99	YOI 2280–99	1982	Leyland Leopard PSU3G/4R	Alexander (B)	B53F	–
259	AXI 2259	1982	Leyland Leopard PSU3E/4R	Wright Royal	C53F	1999
310–19	AXI 310–19	1982	Leyland Leopard PSU3F/4R	Alexander (B)	B53F	–
320–39	BXI 320–39	1983	Leyland Leopard PSU3F/4R	Alexander (B)	DP49F	–
2581–600	BXI 2581–600	1982–83	Bristol RELL6G	Alexander (B)	B52F	–
551–54	BXI 5551–54	1983	Leyland Tiger TRCTL11/3R	Duple Caribbean	C51F	1999
555–56	CXI 1555–56	1983	Leyland Tiger TRCTL11/3R	Duple Dominant IV	C53F	1999
340	DXI 3340	1984	Leyland Tiger TRCTL11/2R	Alexander (B) 'N'	DP53F	–
341–59	DXI 3341–59	1984	Leyland Tiger TRBTL11/2RP	Alexander (B) 'N'	DP53F	–
360–69	DXI 3360–69	1984	Leyland Tiger TRBTL11/2RP	Alexander (B) 'N'	C53F [7]	–
370	DXI 3370	1984	Leyland Tiger TRBLXCT/2RP	Alexander (B) 'N'	DP53F	–
371–79	DXI 3371–79	1984	Leyland Tiger TRBTL11/2RP	Alexander (B) 'N'	DP53F	–
541–44	EXI 5541–44	1984–85	Leyland Tiger TRCTL11/3RZ	Wright Contour	C57F	1999
545–48	EXI 5545–48	1984	Leyland Tiger TRCTL11/2RZ	Duple Laser I	C49F	1995–97
549–50	EXI 5549–50	1984	Leyland Tiger TRCTL11/3RZ	Duple Caribbean	C51F [8]	1999
380–88	FXI 380–88	1984	Leyland Tiger TRBTL11/2RP	Alexander (B) 'N'	DP53F	–
399–419	FXI 399–419	1985	Leyland Tiger TRBTL11/2RP	Alexander (B) 'N'	DP53F	–
420–54	GXI 420–54	1985	Leyland Tiger TRBTL11/2RP	Alexander (B) 'N'	DP53F	–
537–38	GXI 537–38	1985	Leyland Tiger TRCTL11/2RZ	Wright Contour	C49F	1994–98
539	GXI 539	1985	Leyland Tiger TRCTL11/3RP	Duple Laser II	C53F	*
540	B 272 AMG	1985	Leyland Tiger TRCTL11/3RH	Wright Contour	C53F	1991

179

Fleet No	Reg No	Built	Chassis type	Body type	Seats	Wdn
536	IXI 1536	1986	Leyland Tiger TRCTL11/3RZ	Duple 320	C55F	2000
600	KXI 600	1986	Volvo B9M	Plaxton Paramount	C39F	–
455–59	GXI 455–59	1986	Leyland Tiger TRBTL11/2RP	Alexander (B) 'N'	DP53F	–
460–69	HXI 460–69	1986	Leyland Tiger TRBTL11/2RP	Alexander (B) 'N'	C53F [9]	–
470–79	HXI 470–79	1986	Leyland Tiger TRBTL11/2RP	Alexander (B) 'N'	DP53F	–
480–99	IXI 1480–99	1986	Leyland Tiger TRBTL11/2RP	Alexander (B) 'N'	DP53F	–
1000–09	IXI 1000–09	1986	Leyland Tiger TRBTL11/2RP	Alexander (B) 'N'	DP53F	–
3011–12	HXI 3011–12	1986	Leyland Lynx LX563TL11	Alexander (B) 'N'	B53F	1989
534–35	JXI 534–35	1987	Leyland Tiger TRCTL11/3RZ	Duple 340	C53F [10]	2000
1010–18	JXI 1010–18	1986	Leyland Tiger TRBTL11/2RP	Alexander (B) 'N'	DP53F	–
1019–39	JXI 1019–39	1987	Leyland Tiger TRBTL11/2RP	Alexander (B) 'N'	DP53F	–
1040–59	KXI 1040–59	1987	Leyland Tiger TRBTL11/2RP	Alexander (B) 'N'	B53F	–
1060–68	KXI 1060–68	1987	Leyland Tiger TRBTL11/2RP	Alexander (B) 'N'	DP53F	–
1069–79	KXI 2069–79	1987	Leyland Tiger TRBTL11/2RP	Alexander (B) 'N'	DP53F	–
1080–99	KXI 2080–99	1987	Leyland Tiger TRBTL11/2RP	Alexander (B) 'N'	B53F	–
1100–14	LXI 1100–14	1987	Leyland Tiger TRBTL11/2RP	Alexander (B) 'N'	DP53F	–
801–04	KXI 7801–04	1987	Mercedes 609D	Ulsterbus	B19F	1996–2000
805–08	LXI 6805–08	1988	Mercedes 609D	Ulsterbus	B19F	1996–97
809–10	LXI 6809–10	1988	Mercedes 609D	Citybus	B19F	2000
1115–29	LXI 1115–29	1988	Leyland Tiger TRBTL11/2RP	Alexander (B) 'N'	B53F	–
1130–39	LXI 1130–39	1988	Leyland Tiger TRBTL11/2RP	Alexander (B) 'N'	C53F	–
1801–04	LXI 4801–04	1988	MCW MF150/50	MCW Metrorider	C21F	1992–96
1140–54	LXI 7140–54	1988	Leyland Tiger TRBTL11/2RP	Alexander (B) 'N'	DP53F	–
1155–79	MXI 3155–79	1988	Leyland Tiger TRBTL11/2RP	Alexander (B) 'N'	B53F	–
811–14	MXI 3811–14	1988	Mercedes 609D	Ulsterbus	B19F	1996–2000
815–22	NXI 815–22	1988	Mercedes 609D	Ulsterbus	B19F	1996–2000
1180–99	NXI 1180–99	1988	Leyland Tiger TRBTL11/2RP	Alexander (B) 'N'	B53F	–
1200–09	NXI 1200–09	1988	Leyland Tiger TRBTL11/2RP	Alexander (B) 'N'	B48F	–

[1] Batch renumbered 1201–70 1969; No 9208 had Willowbrook body; No 9264 was rebodied by Willowbrook after an accident in 1968; No 1258 was rebodied in 1971 using the body off 1209 after two accidents.

[2] No 1372 were reseated DP49F in 1972.

[3] Some were later increased to H48/39F.

[4] Nos 940–50 were originally H48/35F.

[5] Nos 1831–32 were reseated C35F in 1980/82.

[6] Nos 1981–89 were classified PSU3E/4R.

[7] Nos 360–67 were reseated B53F in 1988.

[8] Nos 549–50 were reseated C53F in 1987.

[9] Nos 460/3 were reseated B53F in 1988.

[10] Nos 534–35 were convertible to C57F.

Withdrawal dates of new vehicles (in numerical order)

* Note: Some vehicles shown as transferred to Citybus returned to Ulsterbus in later years. These will be detailed in Volumes 5 and 6 in the series.

Fleet No	Regist No	Withdrawn	Fleet No	Regist No	Withdrawn	Fleet No	Regist No	Withdrawn	Fleet No	Regist No	Withdrawn	Fleet No	Regist No	Withdrawn
101	ROI 101	1982m	153	TOI 153	1987s	216	WOI 2216	1982m	329	BXI 329	1987m	472	HXI 472	1987m
102	ROI 102	1986s	154	TOI 154	1979m	234	WOI 2234	1981m	332	BXI 332	1987m			
103	ROI 103	1987	155	TOI 155	1987s	246	WOI 2246	1986m				483	IXI 1483	1998m
104	ROI 104	1986	156	TOI 156	1982m	255	WOI 2255	1984m	359	DXI 3359	1988m			
106	ROI 106	1982m										487	487 TZ	1976m
110	ROI 110	1981m	160	VOI 160	1980m	264	YOI 2264	1986m	412	FXI 412	1987m	488	488 TZ	1971m
114	ROI 114	1988m	191	VOI 191	1982m	266	YOI 2266	1986m				489	489 TZ	1971m
115	ROI 115	1979m	196	VOI 196	1987m	269	YOI 2269	1985m	445	GXI 445	1986m	490	490 TZ	1978m
143	ROI 143	1982m	197	VOI 197	1986m				453	GXI 453	1988m	491	491 TZ	1980s
			202	VOI 202	1988m	292	AXI 292	1985m				492	492 TZ	1980s
152	TOI 152	1987				310	AXI 310	1983m	471	HXI 471	1987m	493	493 TZ	1980s

Fleet No	Regist No	Withdrawn	Fleet No	Regist No	Withdrawn	Fleet No	Regist No	Withdrawn	Fleet No	Regist No	Withdrawn	Fleet No	Regist No	Withdrawn
			934	COI 934	1985	1212	1212 TZ	1980s	1304	4004 WZ	1984s	1365	BOI 1365	1980m
494	4494 UZ	1981	935	COI 935	1987	1213	1213 TZ	1973m	1305	4005 WZ	1987	1366	BOI 1366	1985s
495	4495 UZ	1981	936	COI 936	1978m	1214	1214 TZ	1978m	1306	4006 WZ	1988	1367	BOI 1367	1985
496	4496 UZ	1976m	937	COI 937	1978m	1215	1215 TZ	1972m	1307	4007 WZ	1985s	1368	BOI 1368	1985
497	4497 UZ	1981	938	COI 938	1978m	1216	1216 TZ	1979s	1308	4008 WZ	1978m	1369	BOI 1369	1986
498	4498 UZ	1975f	941	COI 941	1973m	1217	1217 TZ	1980s	1309	4009 WZ	1976m	1370	BOI 1370	1984
			942	COI 942	1973m	1218	1218 TZ	1980m	1310	4010 WZ	1978m	1371	BOI 1371	1987
501	BOI 1501	1976m	943	COI 943	1973m	1219	1219 TZ	1978s	1311	4011 WZ	1985s	1372	BOI 1372	1976m
502	BOI 1502	1985	944	COI 944	1982m	1220	1220 TZ	1978	1312	4012 WZ	1985s	1373	BOI 1373	1987
503	BOI 1503	1976m	945	COI 945	1986	1221	1221 TZ	1978m	1313	4013 WZ	1988	1374	BOI 1374	1985s
504	BOI 1504	1976m	946	COI 946	1986	1222	1222 TZ	1971m	1314	4014 WZ	1983m	1375	BOI 1375	1984
505	BOI 1505	1976m	947	COI 947	1986	1223	1223 TZ	1977m	1315	4015 WZ	1978m	1376	BOI 1376	1986s
506	BOI 1506	1985	948	COI 948	1988	1224	1224 TZ	1978	1316	4016 WZ	1978m	1377	BOI 1377	1985
507	BOI 1507	1981a	949	COI 949	1982m	1225	1225 TZ	1972m	1317	4017 WZ	1988	1378	BOI 1378	1984m
508	BOI 1508	1976m	950	COI 950	1982m	1226	1226 TZ	1978	1318	4018 WZ	1984s	1379	BOI 1379	1983a
509	BOI 1509	1984				1227	1227 TZ	1978	1319	4019 WZ	1978m	1380	BOI 1380	1986s
510	BOI 1510	1985s	1017	JXI 1017	1988a	1228	1228 TZ	1979	1320	4020 WZ	1985m	1381	BOI 1381	1986
						1229	1229 TZ	1971m	1321	4021 WZ	1984	1382	BOI 1382	1986
511	COI 511	1984s	1062	KXI 1062	1988m	1230	1230 TZ	1979s	1322	4022 WZ	1985	1383	BOI 1383	1988
512	COI 512	1981m				1231	1231 TZ	1972m	1323	4023 WZ	1984s	1384	BOI 1384	1983m
513	COI 513	1982m	1051	9051 UZ	1983m	1232	1232 TZ	1975a	1324	4024 WZ	1978m	1385	BOI 1385	1984
514	COI 514	1982m	1052	9052 UZ	1980m	1233	1233 TZ	1978m	1325	4025 WZ	1974m	1386	BOI 1386	1985
515	COI 515	1982m	1053	9053 UZ	1972m	1234	1234 TZ	1969m	1326	4026 WZ	1976m	1387	BOI 1387	1984m
516	COI 516	1979m	1054	9054 UZ	1978m	1235	1235 TZ	1980s	1327	4027 WZ	1985	1388	BOI 1388	1985
517	COI 517	1985	1055	9055 UZ	1980m	1236	1236 TZ	1979	1328	4028 WZ	1978m	1389	BOI 1389	1986
518	COI 518	1984	1056	9056 UZ	1978m	1237	1237 TZ	1972m	1329	4029 WZ	1978m	1390	BOI 1390	1985
519	COI 519	1984s	1057	9057 UZ	1978m	1238	1238 TZ	1979s	1330	4030 WZ	1980m	1391	BOI 1391	1987
520	COI 520	1986p	1058	9058 UZ	1985p	1239	1239 TZ	1980s	1331	4031 WZ	1976m	1392	BOI 1392	1985p
			1059	9059 UZ	1980m	1240	1240 TZ	1974m	1332	4032 WZ	1978m	1393	BOI 1393	1985
561	XOI 561	1987c	1060	9060 UZ	1973m	1241	1241 TZ	1979	1333	4033 WZ	1985	1394	BOI 1394	1986
562	XOI 562	1987c	1061	9061 UZ	1978m	1242	1242 TZ	1980s	1334	4034 WZ	1982s	1395	BOI 1395	1986
			1062	9062 UZ	1979m	1243	1243 TZ	1972m	1335	4035 WZ	1985	1396	BOI 1396	1986
578	COI 578	1978m	1063	9063 UZ	1973m	1244	1244 TZ	1978m	1336	4036 WZ	1986	1397	BOI 1397	1987s
579	COI 579	1983	1064	9064 UZ	1978m	1245	1245 TZ	1979	1337	4037 WZ	1985p	1398	BOI 1398	1987
580	COI 580	1984	1065	9065 UZ	1976m	1246	1246 TZ	1979s	1338	4038 WZ	1985	1399	BOI 1399	1985
581	COI 581	1983m	1066	9066 UZ	1981m	1247	1247 TZ	1980	1339	4039 WZ	1974m	1400	BOI 1400	1986
582	COI 582	1978a	1067	9067 UZ	1981m	1248	1248 TZ	1979	1340	4040 WZ	1985a	1401	BOI 1401	1988
583	COI 583	1984	1068	9068 UZ	1974m	1249	1249 TZ	1980				1402	BOI 1402	1985m
			1069	9069 UZ	1971m	1250	1250 TZ	1979				1403	BOI 1403	1988
584	584 TZ	1980r	1070	9070 UZ	1973m	1251	1251 TZ	1980s	1341	AOI 1341	1985a	1404	BOI 1404	1977m
585	585 TZ	1979				1252	1252 TZ	1980	1342	AOI 1342	1985	1405	BOI 1405	1986s
586	586 TZ	1976m	1101	4101 UZ	1980	1253	1253 TZ	1980	1343	AOI 1343	1985s			
587	587 TZ	1974	1102	4102 UZ	1980	1254	1254 TZ	1979s	1344	AOI 1344	1978m	1407	BOI 1407	1978m
588	588 TZ	1980s	1103	4103 UZ	1980	1255	1255 TZ	1977s	1345	AOI 1345	1985	1408	BOI 1408	1978m
589	589 TZ	1980s	1104	4104 UZ	1971m	1256	1256 TZ	1980	1346	AOI 1346	1979m	1409	BOI 1409	1987
			1105	4105 UZ	1977	1257	1257 TZ	1978s	1347	AOI 1347	1974m	1410	BOI 1410	1979m
911	COI 911	1986	1106	4106 UZ	1980	1258	1258 TZ	1977m	1348	AOI 1348	1982	1411	BOI 1411	1980m
912	COI 912	1978m	1107	4107 UZ	1972m	1259	1259 TZ	1980c	1349	AOI 1349	1982m	1412	BOI 1412	1986s
915	COI 915	1972m	1108	4108 UZ	1972m	1260	1260 TZ	1979s	1350	AOI 1350	1985s	1413	BOI 1413	1986
916	COI 916	1982m	1109	4109 UZ	1972m	1261	1261 TZ	1976m				1414	BOI 1414	1980m
918	COI 918	1984	1110	4110 UZ	1981a	1262	1262 TZ	1978s	1351	BOI 1351	1986	1415	BOI 1415	1977f
920	COI 920	1981m				1263	1263 TZ	1979	1352	BOI 1352	1982	1416	BOI 1416	1986t
921	COI 921	1986	1201	1201 TZ	1980s	1264	1264 TZ	1979	1353	BOI 1353	1981m			
922	COI 922	1986	1202	1202 TZ	1972m	1265	1265 TZ	1981s	1354	BOI 1354	1984	1417	COI 1417	1986m
923	COI 923	1983	1203	1203 TZ	1979	1266	1266 TZ	1979	1355	BOI 1355	1980m	1418	COI 1418	1974m
926	COI 926	1986	1204	1204 TZ	1976m	1267	1267 TZ	1979	1356	BOI 1356	1985	1419	COI 1419	1985
927	COI 927	1977m	1205	1205 TZ	1979f	1268	1268 TZ	1979u	1357	BOI 1357	1986s	1420	COI 1420	1974m
928	COI 928	1986	1206	1206 TZ	1980s	1269	1269 TZ	1979	1358	BOI 1358	1976m	1421	COI 1421	1987
929	COI 929	1982m	1207	1207 TZ	1971m	1270	1270 TZ	1975a	1359	BOI 1359	1980m	1422	COI 1422	1985m
930	COI 930	1986	1208	1208 TZ	1980s				1360	BOI 1360	1985	1423	COI 1423	1987
931	COI 931	1988	1209	1209 TZ	1970a	1301	4001 WZ	1988p	1361	BOI 1361	1985	1424	COI 1424	1986
932	COI 932	1983	1210	1210 TZ	1976m	1302	4002 WZ	1985	1362	BOI 1362	1988s	1425	COI 1425	1986
933	COI 933	1985	1211	1211 TZ	1971a	1303	4003 WZ	1986s	1363	BOI 1363	1973f	1426	COI 1426	1979m
									1364	BOI 1364	1983	1427	COI 1427	1988

Fleet No	Regist No	With-drawn	Fleet No	Regist No	With-drawn	Fleet No	Regist No	With-drawn	Fleet No	Regist No	With-drawn	Fleet No	Regist No	With-drawn
1428	COI 1428	1986	1490	DOI 3490	1982m	1556	DOI 1556	1986	1629	FOI 1629	1988tp	1690	FOI 1690	1974m
1429	COI 1429	1980m	1491	DOI 3491	1985	1557	DOI 1557	1978m	1630	FOI 1630	1984t	1691	FOI 1691	1985a
1430	COI 1430	1977m	1492	DOI 3492	1986s	1558	DOI 1558	1986s	1631	FOI 1631	1984	1692	FOI 1692	1987t
1431	COI 1431	1986s	1493	DOI 3493	1985m	1560	DOI 1560	1987	1632	FOI 1632	1986	1693	FOI 1693	1977m
1432	COI 1432	1986	1494	DOI 3494	1986	1561	DOI 1561	1987u	1633	FOI 1633	1984s	1694	FOI 1694	1986
1433	COI 1433	1987	1495	DOI 3495	1987s	1562	DOI 1562	1974m	1634	FOI 1634	1984a	1695	FOI 1695	1986m
1434	COI 1434	1981a	1496	DOI 3496	1986	1563	DOI 1563	1976m	1635	FOI 1635	1987	1696	FOI 1696	1987
1435	COI 1435	1987s	1497	DOI 3497	1987	1564	DOI 1564	1976m	1636	FOI 1636	1986r	1697	FOI 1697	1982m
1436	COI 1436	1987	1498	DOI 3498	1982m	1565	DOI 1565	1988	1637	FOI 1637	1985r	1698	FOI 1698	1987
1437	COI 1437	1987s	1499	DOI 3499	1983a	1566	DOI 1566	1988	1638	FOI 1638	1988t	1699	FOI 1699	1986t
1438	COI 1438	1978m	1501	DOI 1501	1988	1567	DOI 1567	1981m	1639	FOI 1639	1987	1700	FOI 1700	1983m
1439	COI 1439	1986	1502	DOI 1502	1985	1568	DOI 1568	1987t	1640	FOI 1640	1984s			
1440	COI 1440	1985s	1503	DOI 1503	1988	1569	DOI 1569	1985	1641	FOI 1641	1985r	1701	HOI 1701	1980f
1441	COI 1441	1988	1504	DOI 1504	1976m	1570	DOI 1570	1982m	1642	FOI 1642	1988t	1702	HOI 1702	1977m
1442	COI 1442	1987s	1505	DOI 1505	1983	1571	DOI 1571	1988	1643	FOI 1643	1983s	1703	HOI 1703	1982m
1443	COI 1443	1984s	1507	DOI 1507	1986	1572	DOI 1572	1981m	1644	FOI 1644	1984m	1704	HOI 1704	1982m
1444	COI 1444	1988s	1508	DOI 1508	1985	1574	DOI 1574	1982m	1645	FOI 1645	1988t	1705	HOI 1705	1982f
1445	COI 1445	1986u	1509	DOI 1509	1977m	1575	DOI 1575	1988s	1646	FOI 1646	1986	1706	HOI 1706	1988r
1446	COI 1446	1987	1510	DOI 1510	1988	1576	DOI 1576	1985s	1647	FOI 1647	1982s	1707	HOI 1707	1982m
1447	COI 1447	1986	1511	DOI 1511	1988s	1577	DOI 1577	1988s	1648	FOI 1648	1984s	1708	HOI 1708	1988t
1448	COI 1448	1987m	1513	DOI 1513	1986	1579	DOI 1579	1987	1649	FOI 1649	1983s	1709	HOI 1709	1976m
1449	COI 1449	1974m	1514	DOI 1514	1987m	1580	DOI 1580	1988	1650	FOI 1650	1981m	1710	HOI 1710	1982
1450	COI 1450	1986s	1515	DOI 1515	1987	1581	DOI 1581	1984m	1651	FOI 1651	1984	1711	HOI 1711	1976m
			1516	DOI 1516	1988	1582	DOI 1582	1987	1652	FOI 1652	1984s	1712	HOI 1712	1981m
1451	DOI 3451	1984m	1517	DOI 1517	1978m	1583	DOI 1583	1986s	1653	FOI 1653	1984u	1713	HOI 1713	1976f
1452	DOI 3452	1987s	1518	DOI 1518	1978m	1584	DOI 1584	1988	1654	FOI 1654	1985	1715	HOI 1715	1980m
1453	DOI 3453	1987s	1519	DOI 1519	1985m	1585	DOI 1585	1986s	1655	FOI 1655	1983m	1716	HOI 1716	1982r
1454	DOI 3454	1986	1520	DOI 1520	1987u	1586	DOI 1586	1988	1656	FOI 1656	1974m	1717	HOI 1717	1984r
1455	DOI 3455	1977m	1521	DOI 1521	1987u	1587	DOI 1587	1987a	1657	FOI 1657	1983	1718	HOI 1718	1984a
1456	DOI 3456	1988	1522	DOI 1522	1986	1588	DOI 1588	1986	1658	FOI 1658	1982m	1719	HOI 1719	1988
1457	DOI 3457	1986	1523	DOI 1523	1988	1589	DOI 1589	1988	1659	FOI 1659	1985	1720	HOI 1720	1982m
1458	DOI 3458	1981m	1524	DOI 1524	1988	1590	DOI 1590	1986s	1660	FOI 1660	1983t	1721	HOI 1721	1982m
1459	DOI 3459	1986	1525	DOI 1525	1974m				1661	FOI 1661	1983m	1722	HOI 1722	1987
1460	DOI 3460	1979m	1526	DOI 1526	1987	1592	TOI 3592	1982m	1662	FOI 1662	1984t	1723	HOI 1723	1982r
1461	DOI 3461	1977m	1527	DOI 1527	1988s				1663	FOI 1663	1984t	1724	HOI 1724	1984
1462	DOI 3462	1985	1528	DOI 1528	1986m	1601	FOI 1601	1985	1664	FOI 1664	1974m	1725	HOI 1725	1987
1463	DOI 3463	1987	1529	DOI 1529	1974m	1602	FOI 1602	1985a	as	SOI 6664	1988	1726	HOI 1726	1987
1464	DOI 3464	1987s	1530	DOI 1530	1987a	1603	FOI 1603	1981ut				1728	HOI 1728	1984
1465	DOI 3465	1987	1531	DOI 1531	1976m	1604	FOI 1604	1986r	1665	FOI 1665	1975a	1729	HOI 1729	1974m
1466	DOI 3466	1987a	1532	DOI 1532	1977m	1605	FOI 1605	1981	1666	FOI 1666	1982	1730	HOI 1730	1982a
1467	DOI 3467	1986	1533	DOI 1533	1980m	1606	FOI 1606	1986	1667	FOI 1667	1977a	1731	HOI 1731	1986a
1468	DOI 3468	1986	1534	DOI 1534	1986	1607	FOI 1607	1982s	1668	FOI 1668	1982m	1732	HOI 1732	1986
1469	DOI 3469	1985	1535	DOI 1535	1988	1608	FOI 1608	1988t	1669	FOI 1669	1982m	1733	HOI 1733	1984
1470	DOI 3470	1985s	1536	DOI 1536	1986	1609	FOI 1609	1982s	1670	FOI 1670	1982m	1734	HOI 1734	1986
1471	DOI 3471	1986	1537	DOI 1537	1986	1610	FOI 1610	1981	1671	FOI 1671	1987t	1735	HOI 1735	1983r
1472	DOI 3472	1986	1538	DOI 1538	1986s	1611	FOI 1611	1981	1672	FOI 1672	1988r	1736	HOI 1736	1982f
1473	DOI 3473	1985	1539	DOI 1539	1987	1612	FOI 1612	1979m	1673	FOI 1673	1987	1737	HOI 1737	1982m
1474	DOI 3474	1986u	1540	DOI 1540	1988s	1613	FOI 1613	1974m	1674	FOI 1674	1986	1738	HOI 1738	1982m
1475	DOI 3475	1985s	1541	DOI 1541	1987	1614	FOI 1614	1986	1675	FOI 1675	1987	1740	HOI 1740	1983a
1476	DOI 3476	1984s	1542	DOI 1542	1986	1615	FOI 1615	1977a	1676	FOI 1676	1983m	1741	HOI 1741	1986f
1477	DOI 3477	1978m	1543	DOI 1543	1982m	1616	FOI 1616	1979m	1677	FOI 1677	1985m	1742	HOI 1742	1985u
1478	DOI 3478	1986	1544	DOI 1544	1981m	1617	FOI 1617	1979m	1678	FOI 1678	1982m	1743	HOI 1743	1988
1479	DOI 3479	1985	1545	DOI 1545	1982m	1618	FOI 1618	1978m	1679	FOI 1679	1978m	1747	HOI 1747	1988p
1480	DOI 3480	1986	1546	DOI 1546	1986	1619	FOI 1619	1979m	1680	FOI 1680	1983m	1748	HOI 1748	1981r
1481	DOI 3481	1982m	1547	DOI 1547	1986	1620	FOI 1620	1985t	1681	FOI 1681	1981s	1749	HOI 1749	1988
1482	DOI 3482	1986s	1548	DOI 1548	1987	1621	FOI 1621	1983s	1682	FOI 1682	1977m	1750	HOI 1750	1984
1483	DOI 3483	1986	1549	DOI 1549	1986s	1622	FOI 1622	1983t	1683	FOI 1683	1987	1751	HOI 1751	1981r
1484	DOI 3484	1986s	1550	DOI 1550	1988	1623	FOI 1623	1983t	1684	FOI 1684	1983m	1752	HOI 1752	1986t
1485	DOI 3485	1981m	1551	DOI 1551	1987	1624	FOI 1624	1986r	1685	FOI 1685	1988	1753	HOI 1753	1982r
1486	DOI 3486	1978m	1552	DOI 1552	1987	1625	FOI 1625	1979m	1686	FOI 1686	1988t	1754	HOI 1754	1982m
1487	DOI 3487	1987	1553	DOI 1553	1988	1626	FOI 1626	1979m	1687	FOI 1687	1988t	1755	HOI 1755	1982r
1488	DOI 3488	1988	1554	DOI 1554	1987	1627	FOI 1627	1979m	1688	FOI 1688	1981m	1756	HOI 1756	1982m
1489	DOI 3489	1986s	1555	DOI 1555	1986s	1628	FOI 1628	1979m	1689	FOI 1689	1988	1757	HOI 1757	1988r

Fleet No	Regist No	Withdrawn	Fleet No	Regist No	Withdrawn	Fleet No	Regist No	Withdrawn	Fleet No	Regist No	Withdrawn	Fleet No	Regist No	Withdrawn
1758	HOI 1758	1984r	1806	GOI 1806	1982m	1857	LOI 1857	1978m	2005	JOI 3005	1984m	2244	ROI 2244	1987m
1759	HOI 1759	1988	1807	GOI 1807	1980s	1860	LOI 1860	1988r	2008	JOI 3008	1981m	2245	ROI 2245	1988m
1760	HOI 1760	1978m	1808	GOI 1808	1983s	1861	LOI 1861	1988s	2009	JOI 3009	1976m	2246	ROI 2246	1988c
1761	HOI 1761	1978m	1809	GOI 1809	1976m	1870	LOI 1870	1980m	2010	JOI 3010	1976m	2247	ROI 2247	1988c
1762	HOI 1762	1978m	1810	GOI 1810	1982s	1871	LOI 1871	1978m	2011	JOI 3011	1981m	2248	ROI 2248	1980m
1763	HOI 1763	1984r	1811	GOI 1811	1982s	1872	LOI 1872	1978m	2013	JOI 3013	1978m	2252	ROI 2252	1987m
1765	HOI 1765	1988	1812	GOI 1812	1979a	1873	LOI 1873	1979m	2014	JOI 3014	1983m	2253	ROI 2253	1986m
1766	HOI 1766	1987	1813	GOI 1813	1983s	1879	LOI 1879	1980m	2016	JOI 3016	1982m	2261	ROI 2261	1988c
1768	HOI 1768	1982m	1814	GOI 1814	1981m				2017	JOI 3017	1984m	2263	ROI 2263	1988m
1770	HOI 1770	1982m	1815	GOI 1815	1981	1901	HOI 1901	1979m	2018	JOI 3018	1983m	2265	ROI 2265	1986m
1771	HOI 1771	1982m	1816	GOI 1816	1982s	1906	HOI 1906	1976m	2019	JOI 3019	1983m			
1772	HOI 1772	1976m	1817	GOI 1817	1981m	1907	HOI 1907	1979m	2020	JOI 3020	1980m	2274	TOI 2274	1988c
1773	HOI 1773	1983r	1818	GOI 1818	1981s	1908	HOI 1908	1982m	2021	JOI 3021	1983m	2276	TOI 2276	1987c
1774	HOI 1774	1981m	1819	GOI 1819	1981s	1909	HOI 1909	1986	2023	JOI 3023	1981m	2278	TOI 2278	1981m
1775	HOI 1775	1982r	1820	GOI 1820	1980s	1910	HOI 1910	1985	2024	JOI 3024	1982m	2287	TOI 2287	1987c
1776	HOI 1776	1976m	1821	GOI 1821	1981s	1911	HOI 1911	1986	2025	JOI 3025	1985m	2288	TOI 2288	1988c
1777	HOI 1777	1984	1822	GOI 1822	1981s	1912	HOI 1912	1986	2026	JOI 3026	1987m	2289	TOI 2289	1987c
1778	HOI 1778	1986	1823	GOI 1823	1981s	1914	HOI 1914	1977m	2028	JOI 3028	1983m	2295	TOI 2295	1986m
1779	HOI 1779	1987	1824	GOI 1824	1982	1929	HOI 1929	1976m	2030	JOI 3030	1976m	2296	TOI 2296	1988c
1780	HOI 1780	1988	1825	GOI 1825	1983s	1930	HOI 1930	1975m	2032	JOI 3032	1987m	2297	TOI 2297	1988c
1781	HOI 1781	1981a				1931	HOI 1931	1976m	2036	JOI 3036	1988m	2299	TOI 2299	1988c
1782	HOI 1782	1986				1933	HOI 1933	1978m	2039	JOI 3039	1987m	2301	TOI 2301	1987c
1783	HOI 1783	1981m	1830	POI 9830	1980s				2040	JOI 3040	1976m	2303	TOI 2303	1981m
1784	HOI 1784	1984r				1937	KOI 9937	1982m						
1785	HOI 1785	1977m	1831	LOI 1831	1986t	1942	KOI 9942	1981m	2121	MOI 2121	1978m	2361	UOI 2361	1988c
1786	HOI 1786	1985a	1832	LOI 1832	1985t	1946	KOI 9946	1978m	2122	MOI 2122	1981m	2362	UOI 2362	1988c
1787	HOI 1787	1988m	1833	LOI 1833	1980m	1947	KOI 9947	1978m	2124	MOI 2124	1984m	2363	UOI 2363	1987c
1789	HOI 1789	1982m	1835	LOI 1835	1980m	1949	KOI 9949	1978m	2125	MOI 2125	1983m	2364	UOI 2364	1987m
1790	HOI 1790	1987r	1836	LOI 1836	1988s	1950	KOI 9950	1979m	2130	MOI 2130	1985m	2365	UOI 2365	1988m
1791	HOI 1791	1981m	1838	LOI 1838	1982m	1952	KOI 9952	1978m				2369	UOI 2369	1984m
1792	HOI 1792	1982	1839	LOI 1839	1976m	1953	KOI 9953	1976m	2173	POI 2173	1988c	2370	UOI 2370	1980m
1793	HOI 1793	1988r	1842	LOI 1842	1987	1956	KOI 9956	1979m	2179	POI 2179	1988c	2371	UOI 2371	1984m
1794	HOI 1794	1987	1843	LOI 1843	1987r				2191	POI 2191	1986m	2372	UOI 2372	1980m
1795	HOI 1795	1978m	1844	LOI 1844	1977m	1976	NOI 1976	1979m	2206	POI 2206	1978m	2396	UOI 2396	1981m
1796	HOI 1796	1987	1845	LOI 1845	1987	1977	NOI 1977	1982m	2207	POI 2207	1978m			
1797	HOI 1797	1988	1846	LOI 1846	1981m	1986	NOI 1986	1988m	2209	POI 2209	1978m	2433	WOI 2433	1988c
1798	HOI 1798	1982m	1847	LOI 1847	1987	1987	NOI 1987	1988a	2210	POI 2210	1982m	2442	WOI 2442	1987c
1799	HOI 1799	1981m	1848	LOI 1848	1977m	1988	NOI 1988	1979m				2448	WOI 2448	1982m
			1849	LOI 1849	1981m	1989	NOI 1989	1979m	2232	ROI 2232	1987c			
			1850	LOI 1850	1981m				2236	ROI 2236	1988m	2582	BXI 2582	1986m
1801	GOI 1801	1982	1851	LOI 1851	1977m				2240	ROI 2240	1985m	2585	BXI 2585	1986m
1802	GOI 1802	1982s	1852	LOI 1852	1987	2001	JOI 3001	1978m	2241	ROI 2241	1988c	2586	BXI 2586	1986m
1803	GOI 1803	1982m	1853	LOI 1853	1981m	2002	JOI 3002	1978m	2242	ROI 2242	1988c	2591	BXI 2591	1987c
1804	GOI 1804	1983s	1854	LOI 1854	1981m	2003	JOI 3003	1988m	2243	ROI 2243	1980m			
1805	GOI 1805	1976m	1856	LOI 1856	1985f	2004	JOI 3004	1982m						

Buses destroyed in civil disturbance and rebodied by W Alexander (Belfast)

Leyland Leopards

Fleet No	Destroyed	Rebuilt	Body type	Withdrawn	Fleet No	Destroyed	Rebuilt	Body type	Withdrawn
516	3/1972	6/1976	DP49F	1979m	1400	1/1972	4/1973	DP49F	1986
1303	1/1973	1/1975	B53F	1986	1410	2/1974	7/1976	B53F	1979m
1324	7/1972	3/1973	DP49F	1978m	1419	11/1971	3/1973	B53F	1985
1336	1/1972	2/1974	B53F	1986	1420	2/1974	9/1979	B53F	1982m (rebuilt as 1592)
1347	10/1974	9/1978	B53F	1989 (rebuilt as 1591)	1423	1/1972	4/1973	DP49F	1987
1371	2/1973	2/1974	B53F	1987	1428	1/1972	2/1973	DP49F	1986
1373	4/1972	8/1973	DP49F	1987	1429	1/1972	2/1973	DP49F	1980m
1380	3/1972	7/1973	DP49F	1986	1432	11/1973	1/1975	B53F	1986
1383	11/1973	5/1976	B53F	1988	1438	2/1973	6/1976	B53F	1978m
1394	11/1977	2/1974	B53F	1986	1441	11/1971	2/1973	B53F	1988
1398	10/1971	5/1973	DP49F	1987	1455	7/1972	4/1973	B53F	1977m

Fleet No	Destroyed	Rebuilt	Body type	Withdrawn
1474	2/1973	6/1976	B53F	1986
1477	7/1972	2/1974	B53F	1978m
1488	1/1974	6/1976	B53F	1988
1504	12/1972	7/1974	B53F	1976m
1506	4/1973	3/1974	B53F	–

Fleet No	Destroyed	Rebuilt	Body type	Withdrawn
1512	10/1972	5/1976	B53F	–
1525	6/1972	3/1973	B53F	1974m
1547	1/1974	9/1978	B53F	1986
1555	9/1972	7/1974	B53F	1986

Bristol LH

Fleet No	Destroyed	Rebuilt	Body type	Withdrawn
1664	10/1974	2/1979	B45F	1988
1692	10/1974	12/1978	B45F	1987

Bristol RELL

Fleet No	Destroyed	Rebuilt	Body type	Withdrawn
2261	8/1982	6/1983	B52F	1988c
2262	5/1982	3/1983	B52F	–

(3) Flexibus Minibuses built 1984–88

Fleet No	Reg No	Built	Chassis type	Converter/Body	Seats	Wdn
1	DXI 9001	1984	Mercedes 609D	Reeve Burgess	C19F	1996
2–3	EXI 9002–03	1985	Mercedes 609D	PMT	C19F	1998
4	GXI 5004	1985	Talbot Express	Wright	C12F	1991
5	GXI 5005	1985	Renault Traffic Master	Wright	C13F	1994
6	GXI 5006	1985	Mercedes 307D	Wright	C12F	1997
7	HXI 4007	1985	Mercedes 608D	Ulsterbus	C19F	1996
8–9	HXI 6008–09	1986	Mercedes 608D	Ulsterbus	C19F	1996–99
10	HXI 6010	1986	Renault Traffic Master	Ulsterbus	C13F	1995
11–12	IXI 1111–12	1986	Mercedes 608D	Ulsterbus	C19F	1996
13–14	IXI 3113–14	1986	Mercedes 608D	Ulsterbus	C19F	1996–97
15–16	IXI 7015–16	1987	Mercedes 608D	Ulsterbus (tail lift)	C18F	2000
17–20	IXI 7017–20	1986	Iveco 60.10V	Ulsterbus	C19F	1991
21–22	JXI 221–22	1987	Renault Traffic Master	Ulsterbus	C13F	1997
23–25	JXI 223–25	1986	Mercedes 609D	Ulsterbus	C19F	1996–97
26	JXI 226	1987	Mercedes 609D	Ulsterbus (tail lift)	C18F	–
27–30	KXI 1027–30	1987	Mercedes 609D	Ulsterbus	C19F	2000
32	LXI 1032	1987	Mercedes 609D	Ulsterbus	C19F	2001
33–35	LXI 1033–35	1988	Mercedes 609D	Ulsterbus	C19F	1997
36–37	LXI 1036–37	1988	Mercedes 609D	Citybus	C19F	–

(4) Pre-owned vehicles acquired by Ulsterbus 1967–1988

For details of registration numbers, etc, see the withdrawal list at the end of this section.

Fleet No	Reg No	Into service	New	Chassis type	Body type	Seats	Wdn
Ex-6th Newtownards Sea Scouts in 1970 (originally Edinburgh Corporation)							
541	NFS 749	1970	1955	Ley Tiger Cub PSUC1/5	Alexander (F)	DP41F	1973
Ex-Ford Motor Co demonstrator in 1970							
1100	CNO 797 G	1971	1970	Ford R192	Willowbrook	DP45F	1973
Ex-Leyland Motors demonstrator in 1973							
1600	EOI 8060	1973	1972	Leyland National	integral	B44F	1981
On hire from SMT S&S, Glasgow, in 1973							
8	CTE 888 E	1973	1967	Bedford VAS5	Duple Bella Vista	C29F	1973

Fleet No	Reg No	Into service	New	Chassis type	Body type	Seats	Wdn
Ex-Earnside Coaches, Bridge of Earn in September 1973							
577	HOI 577 [1]	1974	1972	Bedford VAS5	Duple Bella Vista	C29F	1980
Acquired with business of Coastal Bus Services, Portrush in April 1974							
227	WDK 951	–	1960	AEC Reliance 2MU3RP	Duple	C41F	1974
228	2155 VP	1974	1961	AEC Reliance 2MU3RP	Plaxton	C41F	1974
229	327 NMP	1974	1962	AEC Reliance 4MU3RA [2]	Park Royal	B53F	1978
500	AWT 295 B	1974	1964	Leyland Leopard PSU3/3RT	Duple Commander	C51F	1976
599	GVU 453 E	1974	1967	Ford Transit	Martin Walter	C51F	1974
1271–73	various	1974	1964	Bedford VAL14	Duple	C52F	1974
1274	SRN 920	1974	1963	Bedford VAL14	Duple	C49F	1974
1275–76	22–23 JOC	–	1963	Bedford VAL14	Duple	C51F	1974
1298	KTV 175 E	–	1967	Daimler Roadliner SRC6	Marshall	B50F	1974
1299	7901 YZ [3]	1974	1967	Daimler Roadliner SRC6	Marshall	B49F	1974
1300	CIA 3000 [4]	1974	1966	AEC Swift MP2R	Marshall	B48F	1974
9038–40	ECK xxx	–	1952	Leyland Royal Tiger PSU1/13	Leyland	B44F	1974
9041	JWO 122	–	1951	Leyland Royal Tiger PSU1/9	Lyndney	B45F	1974
Ex-London Transport in 1977							
2506–08	VLW xxx G	1977	1968	AEC Merlin 4P2R	Metro-Cammell	B50F	1980
2509–10	AML xxx H	1977	1969	AEC Merlin 4P2R	Metro-Cammell	B50F	1978–80
2511–18	VLW xxx G	1977	1968	AEC Merlin 4P2R	Metro-Cammell	B50F	1978–80
2519–20	AML xxx H	1977	1969	AEC Merlin 4P2R	Metro-Cammell	B50F	1979–80
2521–22	VLW xxx G	1977	1968	AEC Merlin 4P2R	Metro-Cammell	B50F	1977–80
Ex-Citybus Ltd, Belfast, in 1977							
2704–06	1704–06 MZ	1977	1964	Leyland Atlantean PDR1/1	MH Coachworks	H44/34F	1978–79
2707/9	707/9 UZ	1977	1967	Daimler CRG6	Potter	H44/30F	1978
2725–30	725–30 UZ	1977	1967	Daimler CRG6	Potter	H44/30F	1978–82
Ex-Weatherdair, Ballywalter, in November 1977							
576	MTV 47 P	1978	1976	Bedford VAS5	Duple Baby Dominant	C29F	1980
Ex-Citybus Ltd, Belfast, in 1978							
2716	716 UZ	1978	1967	Daimler Fleetline CRG6	Alexander (B)	H44/31F [5]	1993
2712/8/9	712/8/9 UZ	1978	1967	Daimler Fleetline CRG6	Potter	H44/30F	1980–82
2722–23	722–23 UZ	1978	1967	Daimler Fleetline CRG6	Potter	H44/30F	1979–80
Ex-London Transport (via Citybus Ltd) in 1978							
2490–92/4	VLW xxx G	1978	1969	AEC Merlin 4P2R	Metro-Cammell	B25D	1980
2496–97	AML xxx H	1978	1969	AEC Merlin 4P2R	Metro-Cammell	B25D	1980
Ex-Grey Green Travel, London, in May 1978							
569–71	EMD xxx J	1978	1971	Leyland Leopard PSU3B/4R	Plaxton Elite	C53F	1983–85
572–73	EMD xxx J	1978	1971	Leyland Leopard PSU3B/4R	Plaxton Elite	C49F	1984
574	GGH 612 J	1978	1971	Leyland Leopard PSU3B/4RT	Plaxton Elite	C53F	1983
575	XJH 429 K	1978	1971	Leyland Leopard PSU5/4R	Plaxton Elite	C57F	1984
Ex-London Transport (via Citybus Ltd) in 1978							
4	EGN 206 J	1978	1970	AEC Swift 4MP2R/1	Marshall	B32D	1980
7	EGN 374 J	1978	1970	AEC Swift 4MP2R/1	Park Royal	B32D	1979

Fleet No	Reg No	Into service	New	Chassis type	Body type	Seats	Wdn
12–15	EGN xxx J	1978	1971	AEC Swift 4MP2R/1	Metro-Cammell	B32D	1978–80
17–18, 25	EGN xxx J	1978	1971	AEC Swift 4MP2R/2	Metro-Cammell	B32D	1980–81
26	EGN 660 J	1978	1971	AEC Swift 4MP2R/3	Metro-Cammell	B32D	1980

Ex-Southdown Motor Services, Brighton, in March 1979

1187–89	EUF xxx D	1979	1966	Leyland Leopard PSU3/1R	Weymann	B53F	1980–81
1190–93	HUF xxx E	1979	1967	Leyland Leopard PSU3/4RT	Marshall	B53F	1981–82
1194–99	KCD xxx F	1979	1968	Leyland Leopard PSU3/4RT	Marshall	B53F	1980–81

Ex-British Airways, London, in April 1979

951–54	LYF xxx D	1979	1966	Leyland Atlantean PDR1/1	MCW	H40/29F [6]	1982–83

Ex-Ribble Motor Services, Preston, in July 1979

1141–50	CRN xxx D	1979	1966	Leyland Leopard PSU3/4RT	Marshall	DP49F	1981–85

Ex-Southdown Motor Services, Brighton, in September 1979

1168	HUF 766 F	1979	1967	Leyland Leopard PSU3/4RT	Marshall	B53F	1981
1169–83	KCD xxx D	1979-80	1968	Leyland Leopard PSU3/4RT	Marshall	B53F	1979–81
1184–86	KUF xxx F	1979	1968	Leyland Leopard PSU3/4R	Willowbrook	B53F	1980–81

Ex-Ribble Motor Services, Preston, in March 1980

1129–40	DRN xxx D	1981–82	1966	Leyland Leopard PSU3/4R	Marshall	B44F	1981–85

Ex-S & M Coaches, Benfleet, in April 1980

567	REW 987 K	1980	1972	Leyland Leopard PSU5/4R	Plaxton Elite	C57F	1985

Ex-Wilkinson, Hebburn, in April 1980

568	SHN 400 L	1980	1973	Leyland Leopard PSU5/4R	Plaxton Elite	C57F	1986

Ex-Grey Green Coaches, London, in May 1980

566	VLB 666 M	1980	1974	Leyland Leopard PSU5/4R	Plaxton Elite	C57F	1989

Ex-Coalisland Construction Co, in April 1981

–	KJM 3	–	1963	Bedford SB	Plaxton	C41F	1981

Ex-Strathclyde PTE, Glasgow, in 1982–83

955–56	MDS xxx P	1982	1976	Leyland Atlantean AN68A/1R	Alexander (F)	H45/31F	1987–92
957–62	KSU xxx P	1982	1975	Leyland Atlantean AN68A/1R	Alexander (F)	H45/31F	1986–92
963–64	various	1982	1975	Leyland Atlantean AN68/1R	Alexander (F)	H45/31F	1987–90
965–68	GGG xxx N	1982–83	1974	Leyland Atlantean AN68/1R	Alexander (F)	H45/31F	1986–90
969–70	KSU xxx P	1982–83	1975	Leyland Atlantean AN68A/1R	Alexander (F)	H45/31F	1983–88
971–73	various	1983	1975	Leyland Atlantean AN68/1R	Alexander (F)	H45/31F	1983–92
974–79	various	1983–84	1974	Leyland Atlantean AN68/1R	Alexander (F)	H45/31F	1983–91

Ex-West Yorkshire Road Car in 1983

752/3/5	various	1983	1972	Bristol RELL6G	ECW	B53F	1983–88
754	VWT 683 L	1983	1973	Bristol RELL6G	ECW	B53F	1984
756	LWU 543 K	1983	1971	Bristol RELL6G	ECW	B53F	1984
765–67	OWY xxx K	1983	1972	Bristol RESL6G	ECW	B47F	1984–85

Ex-United Automobile Services, Darlington, in December 1984

782–83	OHN xxx L	1985	1972	Bristol RELL6G	ECW	B50F	1986–87

Fleet No	Reg No	Into service	New	Chassis type	Body type	Seats	Wdn
786–87	GHN xxx J	1985	1971	Bristol RESL6G	ECW	B45F	1985–87

Ex-Eastern National Omnibus Co, Chelmsford, in February 1985

788	LVX 116 J	1985	1970	Bristol RELL6G	ECW	B53F	1986
789	MHK 914 J	1985	1971	Bristol RELL6G	ECW	B53F	1989
795–96	WNO xxx L	1985	1972	Bristol RELL6G	ECW	B53F	1986–88

Ex-Craiggs, Amble, in June 1985

565	AJD 165 T	1985	1979	Leyland Leopard PSU4E/4R	Plaxton Supreme	C41F [7]	1992

Acquired with business of Tyme Taxis, Carrickfergus, in June 1985

–	VVU 760 L	–	1973	AEC Reliance	Caetano	C51F	1985
–	UCK 533	–	1963	Leyland Leopard PSU3/1R	Marshall	B53F	1985
–	UIA 4284	–	1972	Bedford YRQ	Plaxton	C45F	1985
–	NWX 434 K	–	1972	Bedford YRQ	Plaxton	C45F	1985

Ex-Proctor, Fenton, in August 1985

576	AJD 166 T	1985	1979	Leyland Leopard PSU4E/4R	Plaxton Supreme	C41F [8]	1992

Ex-Lothian Region Transport, Edinburgh, in Dec 1985–Jan 1986

900/3	WFS xxx K	1986	1972	Leyland Atlantean PDR1A/1	Alexander (F)	H45/33F	1986
901–02	WFS xxx K	–	1972	Leyland Atlantean PDR1A/1	Alexander (F)	H45/30D	1989
979–89	SSF xxx H	1986–88	1970	Leyland Atlantean PDR1A/1	Alexander (F)	H45/33F	1986–89
990–92	WFS xxx K	–	1972	Leyland Atlantean PDR1A/1	Alexander (F)	H45/30D	1989
993–95	WFS xxx K	1986–89	1971	Leyland Atlantean PDR1A/1	Alexander (F)	H45/33F	1987–89
996–99	WFS xxx K	1986–90	1972	Leyland Atlantean PDR1A/1	Alexander (F)	H45/33F	1986–89

Ex-Ribble Motor Services, Preston, in April 1986

719–20	OCK xxx L	1986	1971	Bristol RESL6L	ECW	B47F	1987
721–23	NCK xxx J	1986	1971	Bristol RESL6L	ECW	B47F	1988–89

Ex-Citybus Ltd, Belfast, in April 1986

2893	JOI 2893	1982	1976	Leyland Atlantean AN68/2R	Alexander (B)	H49/37F [9]	1995

Acquired with business of Sureline Coaches, Lurgan, in June 1987

31	CDZ 6664	1987	1987 [10]	Mercedes 709D	Wright	C20F	2002
669	4003 WZ	1987	1969	Leyland Leopard PSU3A/4R	Alexander (B)	B53F	1988
670–72	4004/11/2 WZ	1987	1969	Leyland Leopard PSU3A/4R	Potter	B53F	1987–88
673	4023 WZ		1969	Leyland Leopard PSU3A/4R	Potter	DP49F	1987
674	BOI 1510	–	1970	Leyland Leopard PSU3A/4RT	Alexander (B)	DP49F	1987
675	BOI 1374	1987	1970	Leyland Leopard PSU3A/4R	Alexander (B)	DP49F	1988
676–77	COI 511/9	–	1971	Leyland Leopard PSU3B/4RT	Alexander (B)	DP49F	1987–88
678–79	COI 1431/43	1987	1971	Leyland Leopard PSU3B/4R	Alexander (B)	B53F	1987–88
680	DOI 3470	1987	1971	Leyland Leopard PSU3B/4R	Alexander (B)	DP49F	1988
681	DOI 1555	1987	1972	Leyland Leopard PSU3B/4R	Alexander (B)	B53F	1988
682–89	FOI xxxx	–	1973	Bristol LH6L	Alexander (B)	B45F	1987
690	HIB 9642 [11]	1987	1978	Bedford YNT	Plaxton	C53F	1989
691	NKK 920 P	1987	1976	Bedford YRT	Caetano	C53F	1987
692	CIB 5936	1987	1977	Ford R1014	Plaxton	C45F	1987
693	FIB 2462 [12]	1987	1977	Ford R1114	Caetano	C53F	1987
694	DIB 2835	1987	1979	Ford R1114	Duple	C53F	1989

187

Fleet No	Reg No	Into service	New	Chassis type	Body type	Seats	Wdn
695	FIB 4533 [13]	1987	1980	Ford R1114	Plaxton	C53F	1990
696	FIB 8279 [14]	1987	1980	Ford R1114	Duple	C53F	1990
697	HIB 9482 [15]	1987	1982	DAF MB200	Plaxton Viewmaster	C51F	1999
698	HIB 2138	1987	1984	Ford R1014	Sureline/Wright	C45F	1987

Ex-Midland Red South in May 1988

| 1893–900 | JHA xxx L | – | 1973 | Leyland Leopard PSU3B/4R | Marshall | B53F [16] | 1987–92 |

Ex-Northern Scotish in September 1988

| 1887–90 | RAG xxx M | – | 1973–74 | Leyland Leopard PSU3/3R | Alexander 'Y' | B53F [17] | – |

Ex-Clydeside Scottish in September 1988

| 1884-6/91 | OSJ xxx R | – | 1976 | Leyland Leopard PSU3/3R | Alexander 'Y' | B53F [17] | – |
| 1892 | SHS 962 M | 1988 | 1974 | Leyland Leopard PSU3B/4R | Willowbrook | B53F | 1989 |

[1] No 577 was previously registered TPT 445 K.
[2] No 229 was originally an AEC demonstrator.
[3] No 1299 was previously registered KVT 173 E.
[4] No 1300 was originally an AEC demonstrator LYY 827 D.
[5] No 2716 was converted to OT44/31F in 1981.
[6] Nos 951–54 were originally CH38/16F.
[7] No 565 was reseated as C35F in 1985 and reverted to C41F in 1988.
[8] No 576 was reseated as C39F in 1985

[9] No 2893 was converted to OT49/37F in 1986.
[10] No 31 had not operated with Sureline.
[11] No 690 was previously registered ARB 522 T.
[12] No 693 was previously registered AFM 201 S.
[13] No 695 was previously registered CAX 17 V.
[14] No 696 was previously registered FCP 622 W.
[15] No 697 was previously registered WNR 118 X.
[16] Nos 1893/5–7 were B49F.
[17] Purchased only for driver training.

Withdrawal dates of pre-owned vehicles

Fleet No	Regist No	Withdrawn	Fleet No	Regist No	Withdrawn	Fleet No	Regist No	Withdrawn	Fleet No	Regist No	Withdrawn	Fleet No	Regist No	Withdrawn
4	EGN 206J	1980c	599	GVU 453E	1974s	720	OCK 351K	1987m	964	HGG 247N	1987	1132	DRN 670D	n/o
7	EGN 374J	1979	669	4003 WZ	1988	723	NCK 334J	1988c	967	GGG 307N	n/o	1133	DRN 674D	1983m
8	CTE 888E	1973s	670	4004 WZ	n/o	752	MWW 753K	1984m	968	GGG 308N	1986	1134	DRN 675D	1982m
12	EGN 559J	1978	671	4011 WZ	1988	753	MWW 754K	1983m	969	KSU 849P	1988	1135	DRN 677D	1981m
13	EGN 560J	1980c	672	4012 WZ	1988	754	VWT 683L	1984m	970	KSU 852P	1983m	1136	DRN 678D	1982m
14	EGN 561J	1980m	673	4023 WZ	n/o	755	TWX 197L	1988m	973	JGA 197N	1983	1137	DRN 679D	1982m
15	EGN 562J	1979c	674	BOI 1510	n/o s	756	LWU 543K	1984m	974	JGA 727N	1984	1138	DRN 680D	1982
17	EGN 579J	1980c	675	BOI 1374	1988	765	OWY 749K	1985m	976	OYS 201M	1988	1139	DRN 681D	n/o
18	EGN 608J	1980c	676	COI 511	1988	766	OWY 751K	1984m	977	OYS 205M	n/o t	1140	DRN 682D	1983m
25	EGN 594J	1980c	677	COI 519	n/o s	767	OWY 752K	1984m	978	RGB 600M	n/o	1141	CRN 818D	1985
26	EGN 660J	1979	678	COI 1431	1988	782	OHN 459L	1986m	979	RGB 602M	n/o	1142	CRN 819D	1981
227	WDK 951	n/o	679	COI 1443	1987s	783	OHN 460L	1987m	980	SSF 376H	n/o	1143	CRN 821D	1981
228	2155 VP	n/o	680	DOI 3470	1988	786	GHN 445J	1987m	982	SSF 382H	n/o	1144	CRN 822D	1981m
229	327 NMP	1978	681	DOI 1555	1988	787	GHN 446J	1985m	985	SSF 399H	n/o	1145	CRN 824D	1982m
500	AWT 295B	1976s	682	FOI 1607	n/o	788	LVX 116J	1986m	986	SSF 386H	n/o	1146	CRN 827D	1983
541	NFS 749	1973a	683	FOI 1621	n/o s	795	WNO 539L	1988m	987	SSF 387H	n/o	1147	CRN 828D	1982m
567	REW 987K	1985	684	FOI 1634	n/o	796	WNO 540L	1986m	989	SSF 389H	n/o s	1148	CRN 829D	1981m
568	SHN 400L	1986	685	FOI 1643	n/o	901	WFS 283K	n/o	990	WFS 288K	n/o s	1149	CRN 830D	1981a
569	EMD 607J	1985	686	FOI 1647	n/o	902	WFS 287K	n/o	991	WFS 291K	n/o	1150	CRN 831D	1982m
570	EMD 608J	1984	687	FOI 1648	n/o s	951	LYF 306D	1983	992	WFS 291K	n/o	1168	HUF 766E	1981
571	EMD 609J	1983	688	FOI 1649	n/o	952	LYF 312D	1982m	993	WFS 273K	n/o	1169	KCD 170F	1980
572	EMD 610J	1984	689	FOI 1681	n/o s	953	LYF 315D	1983t	994	WFS 274K	1987a	1170	KCD 172F	1980
573	EMD 611J	1984	691	NKK 920P	1987s	954	LYF 318D	1983t	997	WFS 277K	n/o t	1171	KCD 176F	1981
574	GGH 612J	1983	692	CIB 5936	1987	955	MDS 668P	1987	1100	CNO 797G	1973	1172	KCD 177F	1981
575	XJH 429K	1984	693	FIB 2462	1987	958	KSU 867P	1986	1129	DRN 661D	n/o	1173	KCD 178F	n/o
576	MTV 47P	1980s	698	HIB 2138	1987s	959	KSU 869P	1988s	1130	DRN 666D	1983m	1174	KCD 180F	1981
577	HOI 577	1980s	719	OCK 346K	1987m	962	KSU 875P	1988	1131	DRN 667D	1985	1175	KCD 181F	1981

Fleet No	Regist No	Withdrawn	Fleet No	Regist No	Withdrawn	Fleet No	Regist No	Withdrawn	Fleet No	Regist No	Withdrawn	Fleet No	Regist No	Withdrawn
1176	KCD 182F	1981m	1194	KCD 173F	1981	1895	JHA 216L	n/o s	2516	VLW 362G	1979m	2726	726 UZ	1981
1177	KCD 183F	1981	1195	KCD 174F	1980	1896	JHA 219L	n/o s	2517	VLW 364G	1980c	2727	727 UZ	1982
1178	KCD 184F	1981	1196	KCD 175F	1981	1897	JHA 235L	n/o s	2518	VLW 387G	1980c	2728	728 UZ	1978m
1179	KCD 185F	1983	1197	KCD 189F	1981	1898	JHA 239L	n/o s	2519	AML 651H	1980	2729	729 UZ	1981s
1180	KCD 186F	1981	1198	KCD 190F	1981	1899	JHA 240L	n/o s	2520	AML 652H	1979m	2730	730 UZ	1978
1181	KCD 187F	1981	1199	KCD 191F	1981m	1900	JHA 248L	n/o s	2521	VLW 329G	1977m	9038	ECK 562	n/o
1182	KCD 188F	1981	1271	CTD 324B	1974s	2490	VLW 460G	1980c	2522	VLW 366G	1980c	9039	ECK 577	1974p
1183	KCD 193F	1981m	1272	BWE 755B	1974	2491	VLW 461G	1980	2704	1704 MZ	1978	9040	ECK 586	n/o r
1184	KUF 203F	1980s	1273	AWT 351B	1974s	2492	VLW 465G	1980	2705	1705 MZ	1978	9041	JWO 122	n/o r
1185	KUF 204F	1981	1274	SRN 920	1974s	2494	VLW 527G	1978m	2706	1706 MZ	1979	–	KJM 3	n/o
1186	KUF 205F	1981	1275	22 JOC	n/o	2496	AML 548H	1973	2707	707 UZ	1978m	–	VVU 760L	n/o
1187	EUF 141D	1980s	1276	23 JOC	n/o			n/o m	2709	709 UZ	1978m	–	UCK 533	n/o
1188	EUF 142D	1981	1298	KVT 175E	n/o c	2497	AML 576H	1980c	2712	712 UZ	1982t	–	UIA 4284	n/o
1189	EUF 145D	1981	1299	7901 YZ	n/o c	2511	VLW 346G	1980c	2718	718 UZ	1981	–	NWX 434K	n/o
1190	HUF 765E	1981	1300	CIA 3000	1974c	2512	VLW 352G	1980c	2719	719 UZ	1980			
1191	HUF 767E	1982	1600	EOI 8060	1981	2513	VLW 353G	1980c	2722	722 UZ	1979			
1192	HUF 768E	1982	1893	JHA 214L	n/o s	2514	VLW 354G	1978m	2723	723 UZ	1980			
1193	HUF 769E	1982	1894	JHA 215L	n/o s	2515	VLW 356G	1980	2725	725 UZ	1979			

Vehicles allocated for staff transport (Duncrue Street and Milewater Road) – in chronological order:

642	1/1975– 5/1975	309	8/1977– 1/1979	798	8/1980– 10/1981t
874	6/1975– 10/1975	815	1/1979– 4/1979	1133	11/1981– 4/1982
376	10/1975– 5/1976	951	6/1979 (1 week)	1603	5/1982– 5/1984
1028	5/1976– 10/1976	952	6/1979– 10/1979	1653	6/1984– 10/1985
1039	11/1976– 1/1977	1268	11/1979– 3/1980	1742	10/1985– 1/1986
308	1/1977– 7/1977m	454	3/1980– 11/1981	1445	2/1986– 5/1986

1474	7/1986– 8/1986
1520	9/1986– 4/1987
1561	4/1987 (1 week)
1521	11/1987– 10/1989

Vehicles retained for towing after withdrawal

Leyland PS1 & PS2

502	4/1967–10/1969	LD
(7)515	4/1967– 3/1977	LG & DG
(7)571	?/1970–11/1977	LB, NA & SF
572	4/1967– 4/1971	DP
(7)674	4/1967–10/1977	P
7587	4/1967– 4/1971	OM
7840	6/1968– 5/1971	SF
8516	4/1967– ?/1972	NA
8517	4/1967–11/1980	AM
	(last in use)	
8550	6/1968– 5/1971	V
8555	4/1967–10/1971	BM
8578	11/1969– 7/1971	LD
8580	1/1969– ?/1972	NY
8732	4/1967–12/1968	NY
	(Erne colours)	
8860	4/1967– ?/1975	DG
8908	4/1967–10/1971	LR

Leyland PSU (mainly ex Ribble)

8963	5/1973– 3/1974	OM
9005	2/1972– 4/1974	LD
9007	1/1971– 3/1973	M
9008	3/1974– 1/1980	NC/ DP/NA
9010	7/1973– 9/1979	M

9011	5/1971– 5/1978	V
9014	9/1973– 6/1978	NA
9018	10/1971– 3/1979	LR
9026	?/1972– 6/1977	NY
9027	1/1974– 9/1977	LG
9028	2/1972– 6/1980	E
	(last in use)	
9032	10/1971– 2/1980	LB
9033	10/1971–12/1973	SF
9036	10/1971– ?/1976	BM
9037	10/1971– 6/1979	CL
9040	4/1974– 3/1979	LD
	(ex CBS)	
9041	?/1974– 6/1978	OM
	(exCBS)	
9103	4/1971– 8/1973	OM
	(Olympic)	
9104	4/1971– 5/1973	DP
	(Olympic)	

Leyland Leopard L1 (ex WSMT)

527	10/1977– 9/1985	LD, CL, AT
529	9/1979– 1/1987	LB
530	9/1977– ?/1980	NC
531	2/1977?–10/1985	LD
533	10/1977–10/1992	DP
534	1/1978– 3/1983m	OM

535	12/1977– 1/1992	AT
(9)537	11/1977–12/1991	CG
	(last in use)	
538	1/1978– 5/1983	V
(9)540	11/1980– 2/1990	NY

Leyland Tiger Cub PSUC

(9)321	10/1982– 8/1986	NC
	(last of type)	
(9)329	2/1977–10/1982	DG
332	6/1977–11/1980	NY
(9)372	11/1977–12/1982	SF/ OX
(9)427	1/1980–10/1987	BG
	(last of type)	
428	5/1980–12/1984	SS
(9)442	?/1980– 6/1985	BM
(9)453	2/1980– 6/1986	NA
458	4/1981– 2/1985	AD
(9)468	9/1979– 6/1985	M, LR, CL
480	9/1980–11/1985	F

AEC Reliance

(9)291	8/1979–11/1982	LR

Leyland Leopards.

486	11/1980– 4/1982m	AM
584	6/1980– 5/1994	E

Bristol LH6L

1604	7/1987– 1/1989	BG
1624	1/1987– 5/1988	LB
1636	6/1986– 7/1989	NA
1637	6/1986– 7/1995	NC
1641	9/1985– 5/1988	AT
1672	6/1988–11/1988	LB?

Bedford YRQ/YLQ

1706	11/1988– 5/1989	LB
1716	7/1985– 6/1995	AM
1717	12/1984– 9/1994	F
1723	1/1985– 9/1988	LR
1735	4/1983– 1/1992	OM
1/48	8/1982– 7/1991	V
1751	10/1982– 2002	MF
1753	10/1982– 1/1990	DG
1755	11/1982– 3/1988	OX
1758	7/1985– 2/1999	BM
1763	12/1984–12/1993	SS
1773	10/1985–10/1989	LD
1775	10/1982– 4/1985m	AM
1784	12/1984– 1/1993	AD
1790	4/1988– 7/1990	OX
1793	10/1988– 2/1995	LR
1843	5/1988– 1/1994	AT

Leyland PS1 & PS2

501	5/1967–	7/1967
505	10/1967–	9/1968
676	4/1968–	9/1968
7528	11/1967–	1/1968
(allocated but not used)		
7840	3/1967–	8/1969
7841	3/1967–	6/1967
7845	8/1968–	9/1969
8530	11/1967–	1/1968
(allocated but not used)		
8550	9/1967–	4/1969
8565	5/1967–	7/1967
8568	5/1967–	7/1967
8578	11/1967–	11/1969
8580	11/1967–	10/1969
8858	6/1969–	2/1973

Leyland PSU

598	1/1969–	10/1969
(allocated but not used)		

Leyland PD2/10C & PD2/1

606	9/1973–	5/1975
(last of type)		
620	8/1972–	3/1973
642	5/1973–	1/1975
646	9/1972–	3/1974

650	9/1969–	9/1971
652	9/1969–	5/1973
682	3/1970–	9/1973
687	5/1973–	4/1975
706	9/1969–	12/1971
716	9/1969–	1/1972
734	9/1969–	12/1971
759	10/1969–	3/1970
921	11/1967–	6/1968
(allocated but not used)		
930	4/1969–	9/1969
931	4/1969–	9/1969

Leyland PD3

798	4/1982–	4/1985
799	5/1978–	5/1980
801	5/1978–	1/1979
809	5/1978–	11/1980
815	4/1979–	1/1980
819	4/1975–	10/1983
824	4/1975–	10/1983
826	2/1974–	10/1978
829	11/1973–	11/1980
846	7/1982–	9/1985
(last of type)		
849	5/1978–	1/1980
852	11/1978–	6/1982
870	2/1973–	2/1974
876	4/1979–	11/1979

899	4/1975–	5/1981
967	4/1973–	10/1978
974	12/1973–	10/1980
975	1/1975–	5/1975
990	1/1975–	9/1977
994	6/1979–	9/1980

Leyland Atlanteans

953	9/1983–	10/1985
954	9/1983–	2/1987
977	11/1985–	2/1989
997	3/1987–	4/1989

Daimler Fleetline

2712	4/1982–	5/1983

Leyland Tiger Cub

330	4/1977m (1 month)	
348	5/1977–	10/1978
367	10/1973–	3/1977
404	9/1973–	2/1974
440	9/1973	(1 month)

Bristol LH

1603	5/1984–	3/1988
1608	7/1987–	10/1988
(not continuous)		

1620	10/1985	
1622	3/1983–	10/1985
1623	4/1984	(1 month)
1629	7/1987–	1/1994p
(not continuous)		
1630	3/1985–	10/1986
1638	4/1988–	7/1989
1642	8/1988	(1 month)
1645	5/1988–	9/1988
1660	3/1983–	3/1985
1662	2/1984–	1/1986
1663	4/1984–	5/1984
1671	4/1988–	6/1988
1686	2/1988–	11/1988
1687	7/1988–	9/1994
(last of type)		
1692	1/1988–	6/1989
1699	3/1987–	3/1993

Bedford YRQ, YLQ

1708	7/1987–	8/1987
1752	6/1986–	9/1986
1831	1/1986–	3/1994
1832	11/1985–	10/1988

Leyland Leopard

1416	6/1988–	9/1988
1568	11/1987–	11/1990
(Wayfarer training)		

Preserved Ulsterbus vehicles

The list below is of vehicles built new for, or acquired second-hand by, Ulsterbus in the period 1967–88. At the bottom of the opposite page is a list of UTA vehicles which came into preservation via Ulsterbus. This should be treated as an update of the UTA list in Volume 2. Not all vehicles listed are fully restored and some no longer exist, having been subsequently sold or destroyed.

Bristol RELL6L	1058 (1969)
Leyland Leopard PSU3A/4R	1301e, 1337m (both 1969), 1392 (1970)
Leyland Leopard PSU3A/4RT	520 (1971)
Leyland Atlantean PDR2/1	919 (1971)
Leyland Atlantean PDR1A/1	996b (1971 – acquired second hand 1986)
Bristol LH6L	1629 (1973)
Bedford YRQ	1747b (1974)
Leyland Leopard PSU3C/4R	1922, 1926 (both 1975), 1958 (1976)
Bedford YLQ	1859, 1864, 1869 (all 1976)
Leyland Leopard PSU3/3R	1886 (1976 – acquired second hand 1988)
Leyland Leopard PSU3D/4R	1968 (1977)
Bristol RELL6G	2187, 2190 (both 1977), 2386 (1979)
Leyland Leopard PSU3A/4R	1591 (1978)
Leyland Leopard PSU3E/4R	259 (1982)

Meaning of symbols

a	Scrapped after an accident
b	Subsequently sold out of preservation
e	Later scrapped due to serious chassis or body corrosion
f	Destroyed by fire
m	Maliciously destroyed
x	Chassis only exists

In addition to the vehicles listed above and opposite, an ex-NIRTB Bedford OWB was acquired by Ulsterbus in 1985 and reconstructed in the Ulsterbus workshops to its wartime condition as NIRTB No 957 (see pages 167–68)

Ex-UTA vehicles which did not enter the official Ulsterbus fleet.

Leyland Tiger PS1

Fleet No	Regist No	Disposal
(7)489	GZ 6080	T CIE
(7)490	GZ 6081	T
(7)491	GZ 6082	T CIE
(7)492	GZ 6083	T
(7)493	GZ 6084	T CIE
(7)494	GZ 6085	
(7)497	GZ 6088	T CIE
(7)498	GZ 6089	CIE
499	GZ 6090	T
500	GZ 6091	
501	GZ 6092	T t
502	GZ 6093	T r
(7)503	GZ 6094	T CIE
505	GZ 6096	t
510	GZ 6101	T
(7)514	GZ 6105	CIE
515	GZ 6106	T r p
517	GZ 6107	T
519	GZ 6108	T
520	GZ 6111	
521	GZ 6112	
522	GZ 6113	T
523	GZ 6114	T AL
524	GZ 6115	T
525	GZ 6116	
569	GZ 6122	T
570	GZ 6123	T
571	GZ 6124	T r
572	GZ 6125	T r
573	GZ 6126	T CIE
574	GZ6127	
577	GZ 6130	
578	GZ 6131	
579	GZ 6132	
581	GZ 6134	
582	GZ 6135	
583	GZ 6136	
(7)584	GZ 6137	
(7)585	GZ 6138	T CIE
(7)586	GZ 6139	
(7)587	GZ 6140	T r
(7)588	GZ 6141	
(7)589	GZ 6142	
663	GZ 6143	
664	GZ 6144	
665	GZ 6145	
667	GZ 6147	
669	GZ 6149	
670	GZ 6150	
673	GZ 6153	
674	GZ 6154	r
675	GZ 6155	
677	GZ 6157	T
678	GZ 6158	
680	GZ 6160	T CIE
779	GZ 4675	
782	GZ 4678	
7526	GZ 6117	T CIE
7527	GZ 6118	T AL
7528	GZ 6119	T t
7790	GZ 4686	
7797	GZ 4693	T CIE
7800	GZ 4696	T CIE p
7803	GZ 4699	
7804	GZ 4700	
7806	GZ 4702	T CIE
7807	GZ 4703	
7808	GZ 4704	
7811	GZ 4707	T CIE
7812	GZ 4708	
7813	GZ 4709	T CIE
7814	GZ 4710	T CIE
7815	GZ 4711	T CIE
7817	GZ 4713	T AL
7819	GZ 4715	T CIE
7820	GZ 4716	
7821	GZ 4717	
7822	GZ 4718	
7824	GZ 4720	T CIE
7826	GZ 4722	T
7827	GZ 4723	T
7836	GZ 6064	
7840	GZ 6068	t
7841	GZ 6069	t
7844	GZ 6072	CIE
7846	GZ 6074	
7847	GZ 6075	
7848	GZ 6076	
7849	GZ 6077	T
8512	GZ 7580	
8514	GZ 7582	
8516	GZ 7584	r
8517	GZ 7585	r
8520	GZ 7588	JC
8521	GZ 7589	
8526	GZ 7594	
8527	GZ 7595	
8528	GZ 7596	
8530	GZ 7598	T CIE
8531	GZ 7599	
8532	GZ 7600	T CIE
8533	GZ 7601	T
8534	GZ 7602	T
8535	GZ 7603	T CIE
8536	GZ 7604	T
8537	GZ 7605	
8540	GZ 7608	T
8541	GZ 7609	T CIE
8542	GZ 7610	
8543	GZ 7611	T
8544	GZ 7612	T CIE
8546	GZ 7614	
8547	GZ 7615	T CIE
8548	GZ 7616	
8549	GZ 7617	
8550	GZ 7618	T r
8551	GZ 7619	T
8552	GZ 7620	T CIE
8553	GZ 7621	
8554	GZ 7622	T
8555	GZ 7623	T r
8556	GZ 7624	T
8557	GZ 7625	T
8558	GZ 7626	T CIE
8559	GZ 7627	T
8560	GZ 7628	T p
8561	GZ 7629	T
8562	GZ 7630	
8563	GZ 7631	CIE
8564	GZ 7632	
8565	GZ 7633	t
8566	GZ 7634	
8567	GZ 7635	
8568	GZ 7636	t
8570	GZ 7638	CIE
8571	GZ 7639	CIE
8572	GZ 7640	CIE
8573	GZ 7641	T EC
8574	GZ 7642	CIE
8575	GZ 7643	CIE
8576	GZ 7644	
8577	GZ 7645	
8578	GZ 7646	r
8579	GZ 7647	
8580	GZ 7648	r
8581	GZ 7649	
8582	GZ 7650	
8583	GZ 7651	
8584	GZ 7652	CIE
8585	GZ 7653	CIE
8586	GZ 7654	T CIE
8588	GZ 7656	
8589	GZ 7657	EC
8590	GZ 7658	CIE
8591	GZ 7659	
8592	GZ 7660	
8593	GZ 7661	
8594	GZ 7662	
8596	GZ 7664	
8597	GZ 7665	
8598	GZ 7666	
8599	GZ 7667	EC
8645	MZ 316	
8663	MZ 334	
8666	MZ 337	
8730	MZ 1801	
8732	MZ 1803	r

Leyland Tiger PS2

Fleet No	Regist No	Disposal
8812	MZ 1883	T
8828	MZ 1899	T CIE
8829	MZ 1900	T
8859	MZ 1930	CIE
8860	MZ 1931	r
8898	MZ 1969	
8905	MZ 1976	T CIE
8906	MZ 1977	
8907	MZ 1978	
8908	MZ 1979	T r
8909	MZ 1980	T CIE
8910	MZ 1981	T CIE
8911	MZ 1982	T CIE
8912	MZ 1983	
8913	MZ 1984	T
8915	MZ 1986	
8916	MZ 1987	T
8917	MZ 1988	
8918	MZ 1989	
8919	MZ 1990	
8920	MZ 1991	CIE
8921	MZ 1992	CIE
8922	MZ 1993	CIE
8923	MZ 1994	T CIE
8924	MZ 1995	
8925	MZ 1996	T CIE
8926	MZ 1997	CIE
8927	MZ 1998	T
8928	MZ 1999	
8929	MZ 2000	

Leyland Titan PD1

Fleet No	Regist No	Disposal
859	MZ 310	
860	MZ 301	
861	MZ 302	
863	MZ 304	T
864	MZ 305	
867	MZ 308	
868	MZ 309	
908	GZ 3264	
911	GZ 4729	
915	GZ4733	

Disposals:

CIE	CIE hired, later sold
EC	Erne Bus Co, Carrigallen
JC	Jacksons, Cavan
AL	Aer Lingus
r	tow vehicle
t	driver training vehicle
p	preserved
T	These vehicles were still taxed when Ulsterbus took over but were all detaxed by July 1967.

Preserved ex-UTA vehicles

Leyland Tiger PS1:	515, 7800x, 8517, 8520, 8556, 8560, 8570 (all 1947)
Leyland Tiger PS2:	8858 (1949)
Leyland Titan PD2/1:	927 (1950)
Leyland Titan PD2/10c:	659 (1958)
Leyland Titan PD3/4:	815 (1962)
Leyland Tiger Cub PSU1/5T:	301 (1954), 318, 334 (both 1956)
Leyland Tiger Cub PSU1/12:	474a (1962)
AEC Reliance:	234, 236m (both 1963)
Leyland Royal Tiger PSU1/13	9039f (1952 – acquired second hand 1966)